THE SHAKER HOLY LAND

Rare view of Harvard's Shaker Church Family

THE SHAKER HOLY LAND

A Community Portrait

Edward R. Horgan

Foreword by Faith Andrews
Introduction by Robert F. W. Meader

THE HARVARD COMMON PRESS
Harvard, Massachusetts

The Harvard Common Press
The Common, Harvard, Massachusetts 01451

Printed in the United States of America.

Library of Congress Cataloging in Publication Data

Horgan, Edward R.
   The Shaker Holy Land

   Bibliography: p
   Includes index.
   1. Shakers—Massachusetts—History. 2. Massachusetts—Church history. I. Title.
BX9768.H3H67   289'.8'097443   81–20214
ISBN 0–916782–22–0   AACR2

Cover painting by Kathy Jakobsen,
   courtesy of John Jay Gallery, New York,
Cover design by Paul Bacon
Maps by J. Streeter Fowke and Denise Maguire

10 9 8 7 6 5 4 3 2 1

To my family

Contents

Maps

Foreword

MY HUSBAND AND I first met with the Shakers on a fall day in the late 1920s. Searching for early American furniture in the nearby countryside, we were returning from a day's tour. As we approached the Hancock Shaker Village the fragrance of newly baked bread beckoned us, and we stopped to inquire if we could buy a loaf. In a few minutes the sister in charge returned; "Yea, you may have a loaf," she told us. We had embarked on what was to be our life work—a sharing of "the people called Shakers."

Perhaps a personal experience related to Shirley and Harvard might be of interest. It was during a visit to the Ministry at the North Family in New Lebanon that we met Sisters Annie Belle Tuttle and Sadie Maynard, who had been transferred from Shirley and Harvard at the closing of those villages. We visited in the large hall; and their loneliness was apparent as they told us of their earlier lives in Massachusetts. Sister Annie Belle had worked with Eldress Josephine Jilson on a Shaker historical collection, and she had managed to bring some of the material with her to New Lebanon. We were invited to see her museum situated in the basement. While the objects were carefully documented, the darkness and cold was not a welcoming environment. But Sister Annie Belle's enthusiasm was warming, and as we prepared to leave she pressed something into my hand and urged us to return.

Back in our car we were saddened by the encounter, and looked to see what gift Annie Belle had left with us. It was a scrap of blue and white striped linen with a carefully written tag: "a piece of Mother Ann's dress." This was indeed an omen for us.

Today there is a resurgence of interest in the Shaker world. Edward Horgan's book is a timely and welcome contribution to the growing literature on the Shakers. Studies of smaller communities have a way of widening our knowledge of the culture, and give us a deeper insight into the character of its people.

It is appropriate here to quote from a December 12, 1960 letter to us from Thomas Merton: "To me the Shakers are of very great significance, besides being something of a mystery, by their wonderful integration of the spiritual and physical in their work. There is no question in my mind that one of the finest and most genuine religious expressions of the nineteenth century is in the silent eloquence of Shaker craftsmanship."

—Faith Andrews
December, 1981

Acknowledgments

THIS BOOK BEGAN as a one-year digression from another project. Six years of turning over research rocks followed; and during that time, I accumulated a debt to many individuals and institutions. My early interest was nurtured at Fruitlands Museums by William Henry Harrison IV, director until 1979 when Richard S. Reed succeeded him, and by Fruitlands library aide Edee Ryanen. Harvard town historian Elvira L. Scorgie and Shirley historians Lucy P. Longley and Sandy Farnsworth were both gracious and unstinting in rendering assistance. Other key sources for both information and illustrations were Constance (Avery) Thayer, who always seemed to have another box of mementos to search, Erhart Muller and Bayard Underwood, in Harvard, Ralph H. Richardson in Ayer, and Paul Dickhaut and Ray Farrar in Shirley.

Dr. Herbert A. Wisbey, Jr., professor of history at Elmira College, New York, provided inspiration at a Shaker seminar and some early manuscript criticism. Other Shaker scholars consulted include Robert F.W. Meader, Faith Andrews, Charles F. (Bud) Thompson, and Theodore E. Johnson.

The institutions I consulted, besides Fruitlands in Harvard, include the American Antiquarian Society, Berkshire Athenaeum,

Boston Public Library, Canterbury Shaker Village, Fort Devens Museum, Hancock Shaker Community, Library of Congress, Massachusetts Correctional Institution, Massachusetts Historical Society, New York Public Library Manuscripts and Archives Division, New York State Library, Sabbathday Lake Shaker Society, Sawyer Library at Williams College, State Library of Massachusetts, Widener Library at Harvard University, the historical societies and public libraries of Harvard and Shirley, and libraries in the communities of Ayer, Clinton, Fitchburg, Lancaster, Leominster, Littleton, and Worcester.

Hundreds of books, articles, and manuscripts were examined; and because Shaker source material is widely scattered, this required a fair amount of travel and correspondence. Several years of Elder John Whiteley's diaries, for instance, are at Fruitlands, but many others are in the library at Sabbathday Lake. Besides the primary Shaker sources, I found the most helpful resources to be the works of Dr. Edward Deming Andrews and Faith Andrews; the bibliography of Mary Richmond; Clara Endicott Sears's *Gleanings from Old Shaker Journals*; articles by Arthur T. West on the Harvard Shakers and by William Dean Howells on the Shirley Shakers; town histories; and the microfilm collection of the Western Reserve Historical Society in Cleveland, Ohio.

Not only did I have access to manuscript originals, but I also benefited by the earlier labors of reliable copyists. Other researchers were located who had scoured decades of old newspapers.

Several individuals were extremely helpful in arranging for long term loan of source materials and in providing insights into their contents. Chief among the Shaker sourcebooks I consulted were Benjamin Seth Youngs's *Testimony of Christ's Second Appearing*; Calvin Green and Seth Y. Wells's *A Summary View . . .; Rufus Bishop and Seth Y. Wells's Testimonies of the Life . . . of Mother Ann Lee;* Seth Y. Wells's *Testimony Concerning the Character . . . of Mother Ann Lee*, all published during the nineteenth-century Shaker ascendancy; and Anna White and Leila S. Taylor's *Shakerism, Its Meaning and Message*, published in 1904. By then, the Shaker decline was unmistakable.

These books are valuable as official expressions of Shaker belief. Some of the authors were contemporaries of the sect's founders.

But some of these authors contributed as much to the myth as to the reality of the Shaker experience. To get a balanced view of the Shakers, it is necessary to juxtapose the views and accounts of Shaker sources with those of their detractors, such as the hostile Thomas Brown and Amos Taylor, and with more or less impartial observers: the youthful William Plumer, later a congressman; William Bentley, a clergyman; Charles Lane, Transcendentalist philosopher; John Davis Long, educator, and Charles Nordhoff, journalist and sociologist.

Town histories of Harvard and Shirley by Henry Nourse, Seth Chandler, and Ethel Standwood Bolton help to focus the picture. Nourse's *History of Harvard* is preeminent in this category.

Miss Sears, besides possessing a fine, romantic writing style, had the advantage of being an intimate of the last Harvard Shakers. *Gleanings from Old Shaker Journals*, however, is frustratingly undocumented and unindexed. Her Fruitlands colleague, Mr. Harrison, observed of Miss Sears that though she lacked formal scholarship she possessed good intuition.

The People Called Shakers by Edward Deming Andrews and *The Shaker Adventure* by Marguerite Melcher each provide popular and respected accounts of the Shakers. Melcher's book was the first general history of the Shakers in the field, and reflects a personal intimacy and affection for the Canterbury community. Andrews's book is more reserved and more scholarly, but he graciously allows the Shakers to speak for themselves.

The present work owes much to these predecessors and to random other sources. Local newspapers often had choice nuggets of information. But not all insights come from written words and the judgments of others. It was also necessary for the author to walk old Shaker roads, to ramble in overgrown pastures and forest land, to visit Shaker homes and handle artifacts, to kneel at Shaker graves, to listen to the stillness, to imagine, to contemplate. And to do this, it was often necessary to obtain the cooperation of individual and private owners.

For these trespasses and other invasions of people's time and leisure, I acknowledge the following additional individuals: Olive Austin, Wilbur Baldwin, Madelon Bedell, Marilyn A. Boudreau, Leslie C. Bowering, R.J.K. Cahill, Ann Callahan, Tim Carlson,

Tammy Clark, Burton Cofman, Robert Cormier, Paul Cravit, Faith Cross, Anne and Richard DeBoalt, Anna Mary Dunton, Phyllis Farnsworth, Dorothy M. Filley, Mr. and Mrs. Philip J. Finkelpearl, Louise Fletcher, George R. French, Agnes Gleezen, Mr. and Mrs. Kerry E. Gleezen, Esther Gove, Shirley Griffin, Henry Hallowell, Walter Harding, Rev. John U. Harris, Harley Holden, Robert Holden, Gerry Horgan, Herbert H. Hosmer, Shirley Houde, Grace Ingerson, Ralph A. Jilson, Jr., Melvin P. Longley, Sr., Meredith Marcinkewicz, Barbara Masiero, Thomas E. May, Barbara MacKenna, Robert and Terry Moran, Flo Morse, Thomas J. O'Hare, Lisa Parviainen, Archie Patterson, Elmer R. Pearson, Mrs. Charles Perkins, Toby Pirro, Dario Politella, Walter and Mary Roche, Mrs. Frederick C. Sanderson, George Sanderson, Sylvia Shipton, Roger K. Smith, Edward and Amy Squibb, Peter F. Strong, Stephen Swiackey, Emily VanHazinga, Joseph VonDeck, Francis Walett, Mrs. Kaino Waltari Rajala, Andrew and Judy Warner, Gerard C. Wertkin, Mrs. Lillian West, Mrs. Rudolph B. Young, Lydia, Pat, and the Raimo family.

Illustrations were obtained from various institutions and individuals. In addition, the author is indebted to former Congressman Robert F. Drinan, who aided with access to the Library of Congress collections; and to Jim Booth, for photo processing.

Lastly, I thank the Shakers of Canterbury and Sabbathday Lake, whose acquaintance has made the writing of this book a truly inspirational experience.

—E.R.H.

Introduction

THE HARVARD SHAKERS occupy a place unique in the development of the Order—not that the village was the place of origin, which was Niskayuna (Watervliet), nor the first organized, which was New Lebanon (1787), but because it was the community which was first in Mother Ann's heart, and where she probably spent more time than at any other place (with the possible exception of her own home). It was the spot where she and her followers endured more violence than at any other community, even New Lebanon. Adjacent Shirley has to be considered as Harvard's twin; after all, they were only some five miles apart as the crow flies and were later joined into one bishopric.

Harvard had a continuing history of ecclesiastical and communal peculiarities, beginning with Shadrack Ireland, who believed himself immortal and capable of duplicating the resurrection. When Ireland died, both he and his theory disintegrated.

In 1781 Mother Ann and the Elders came to Harvard, apparently drawn thither by the yearning of the people for the salvation promised them by the unfortunate Ireland, and, as at New Lebanon, found a field white for the harvest. And many were gathered in, including Isaac Willard of Harvard and the Wildses of Shirley, all very active in the Order. Later on, Bronson Alcott and his English Mystics established themselves at nearby Fruitlands; and in the 1840s the Millerites were strong, even gathering on a nearby hilltop for their anticipated ascent into the empyrean. In our century, the followers of the reactionary Catholic priest Leonard Feeney, having been excommunicated by the Archdiocese of Boston, established themselves on the edge of the town of Harvard.

But as is now well known, the influence of the Shakers was by no means limited to doctrinal aberrations—though there is strong reason to believe that they influenced, subtly at least, the teachings of Mary Baker Eddy and of Joseph Smith, the Prophet of the Mormons. Mother Eddy, as she was known to her followers (echoes of "Mother" Ann?), taught a divine duality, "our Father and Mother God," as the Scientists' interpretation of the Lord's Prayer phrase it. The Mormons instituted the United Order of Enoch at Kirtland, Ohio in the early days of the church; this was a communal experiment set up along the general lines of the Shaker Order (sans compulsory celibacy) which did not, however, continue for long. Again, there is strong reason to think that the Mormon Church was influenced by the Shakers, for there was much commercial intercourse between Kirtland and the Shaker settlement at North Union, some fifteen miles or so to the west.

Literary luminaries were attracted to the Shaker church, influenced by many aspects of Shaker life. Charles Dickens (who took an excessively dim view of the believers) included a visit to New Lebanon on his way back to New York after a whirlwind tour of the country, curious to see what these peculiar people were like. Mark Twain and Artemas Ward, humorists both, saw them as objects of mirth and ridicule. Hawthorne and Melville saw them in a romantic light, and were interested in their philosophy. William Dean Howells, Catherine Sedgwick, and Kate Douglas Wiggin were entranced with the romantic aspect of the believers' life. The dramatist Samuel D. Johnson was much influenced by the tales of Daniel Pierce Thompson. These are but a few of the many who wrote on various facets of Shaker life and practice. The great Doris Humphrey is known to have drawn heavily on the believers' religious dances for her choreography (although efforts to trace the actual sources for her dance figures have so far proved fruitless). Many musicians have drunk deep from the springs of Shaker song and hymnody, the most prominent among them probably Aaron Copland, whose *Appalachian Spring* is a continuing favorite with concertgoers. Many artists, among them John Warner Barber, Charles Sheeler, and Eric Sloane, have been attracted to the stark beauty of the Shaker villages; Constantine Kermes found a gothic angularity in the members and their garb. Elder Frederick W. Evans of New Lebanon carried on a lively correspondence with Count Leo Tolstoy and tried valiantly to recruit him to the Shaker cause.

As seedsmen, pharmacists, breeders of splendid livestock (they developed the Poland-China hog in Ohio), and manufacturers of fine, if simple, furniture, the Shakers are deservedly famous; and their cabinetry has influenced craftsmen as far afield as Denmark, Sweden, and Japan. Their mechanical ingenuity was and is legendary, though their innocent assumption of being the prime inventors of any number of mechanical devices will not stand up under scholarly scrutiny.

With all this going for them, why have they failed to hold their own numerically? The simplistic explanation is, of course, their firmly held doctrine of celibacy. This is certainly one reason; in Protestant America the appeal of a Protestant monastic order had singularly little impact. Even the Catholic orders have had increasing difficulty in maintaining their strength.

The early nineteenth century was an age of increasing urbanization and industrial proliferation, both basically inimical to a vital interest in religion, especially of the celibate, monastic type. (It must be remembered that, unlike the Catholic, Anglican, and Orthodox religious orders, the Shakers had no body of laity from which to draw; if one were a Shaker at all one was, *ipso facto*, a monastic.) Further, the great days of burning religious fervor, which induced farmers to interrupt their plowing to argue religion over the stone wall, and women to collapse screaming at church for fear of incipient hellfire, had evaporated under the siren calls of Mammon in the shape of the new textile and paper mills, the shipyards, and the lure of overseas trade in exotic ports of the Orient. What lad of spirit in those days could reasonably be expected to stay quietly at home and till his Shaker acres when he would go to sea and behold the "heathen Chinee" in his native habitat, growing rich in the process? It was an exciting, expanding country, filled with unlimited opportunity for those with imagination, determination, and a sense of high adventure—an adolescent America, so to speak, and thus appealing to the young at heart.

Further, fierce, cutthroat economic competition forced the Shaker (and other) handcraftsmen out of business, as did the growth of specialized businesses in agriculture and manufacturing. One of the great sources of recruitment to the Shaker ranks withered on the vine as town and county orphan asylums removed a pool of youngsters which had once filled the believers' Children's Orders. Fewer and fewer men entered the ranks to replace those leaving or dying, with the result that since 1961, with the death of the last Shaker brother in Maine, the Shaker Order has become a sisterhood. (The women always outnumbered the men, a common religious phenomenon.)

Gradually, as numbers diminished, the villages contracted upon themselves and eventually withered entirely away. The first to go was Tyringham, Massachusetts, in 1875, followed in rapid succession by North Union (1889), Groveland (1892), Watervliet, Ohio (1900), Whitewater (1907), Shirley (1908), Pleasant Hill and Union Village (both in 1910), Enfield, Conn. (1917), Enfield, N.H. (1918), Harvard (1918), South Union (1922), Alfred (1931), Watervliet, N.Y. (1938), New Lebanon (1947), and Hancock (1960). Only Sabbathday Lake and Canterbury remain, and only nine Sisters—out of an original high enrollment of around six thousand men, women, and children—remained on the roster in 1981. The late nineteenth and early twentieth centuries were discouraging times indeed.

It is interesting to note what happened to these various defunct communities. Alfred was sold to the Brothers of Christian Instruction (not to be confused with the Christian Brothers, who are also engaged in teaching); Enfield, New Hampshire was obtained by the Brothers of LaSalette, and South Union by the Order of St. Benedict. These last, of all the Catholic orders, are probably closest to the Shakers in philosophy, organization, and works;

even their mottoes, "*Ora et labora*" and "Hands to work, hearts to God" are basically the same. Union Village went to the Otterbein Church, now (thanks to several ecclesiastical mergers) the Methodists. Shirley and Enfield, Connecticut, are state penal institutions. Hancock and Pleasant Hill are museum-restorations, while Watervliet, Ohio was until very recently the farm for a state mental hospital. Its namesake in New York is in part a county home for the indigent, in part the Albany County Airport, and in part privately owned. Harvard, Tyringham, Whitewater, and North Union are in private hands, the remaining buildings owned by various individuals, with the exception of North Union; this property was taken over by the Van Schweringen brothers of railroad fame, who removed all the badly decayed Shaker buildings and sold the land to be developed into a wealthy residential suburb of Cleveland.

The two remaining Shaker villages have lost, or soon will lose, their status as communities wholly owned by their inhabitants. In 1969 Canterbury turned over its property to a self-perpetuating, nonprofit corporation set up to continue the life of the community as an educational institution and museum; the three remaining sisters retain the right of domicile therein so long as they wish. Sabbathday Lake decided in 1981 to do the same thing, with the nine sisters continuing to live in their former home rent free, hostesses to the increasing numbers of visitors who come to them in the season. It is, of course, the hope of the Sabbathday Lake sisters that the unanimous decision by the Parent Ministry in 1965 to close the rolls to further recruitment will be reversed, that new members will be added, and that the Order will be perpetuated—though under the circumstances that would seem to be an exercise in nostalgia and futility. The accumulated funds of the Order already invested, or the income from them, would then very likely be used for various charitable purposes that have been or eventually will be decided upon; no decision has yet been announced.

The remaining Shakers have long felt that while the Order will inevitably disappear physically, its influence and beliefs will continue to prevail and to inspire future generations. After all, the Shaker ideals—peace and harmony, industrious land labor and thriftiness, a firm belief in an Almighty Power, charity and brotherly love—are badly needed in a world torn by strife, contention, greed, and amorality, and increasingly desperate for a better way of life. The Shakers can point the way and provide inspiration (though not necessarily with celibate members) as they did to thousands over the past two centuries.

The increasing attendance at the restored villages and the rapidly growing numbers of books and articles on various facets of the Shaker experience demonstrate the force and viability of the Shaker ethos. As the late Eldress Emma B. King of Canterbury expressed it, "We have been given a trust and have been commissioned as 'Torch Bearers' to help light the way for others. We are not depressed nor defeated as a people, but intend to be true to our trust, valiant to the end with heads lifted, hearts courageous and colors flying. We intend to go down gloriously. Our times are in God's hands. Shakerism is no failure."

—Robert F.W. Meader
Hancock, Massachusetts
October, 1981

Surely God is in this place, pull off your shoes; for the place where ye stand is holy.

—*Secret Book of the Elders*

The Shaker Holy Land

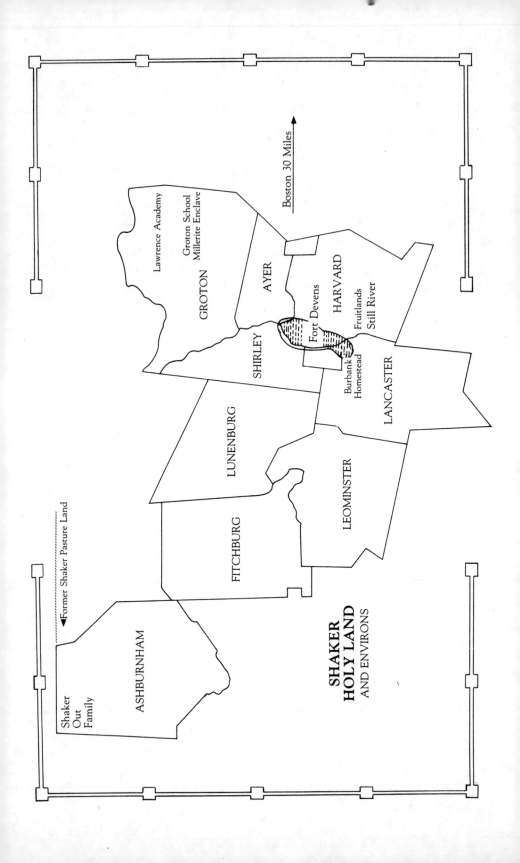

SHAKER HOLY LAND AND ENVIRONS

Former Shaker Pasture Land

Shaker Out Family

ASHBURNHAM

FITCHBURG

LUNENBURG

LEOMINSTER

LANCASTER

SHIRLEY

GROTON

Lawrence Academy

Groton School
Millerite Enclave

AYER

Fort Devens

HARVARD

Burbank Homestead

Fruitlands
Still River

Boston 30 Miles

1. Overview:
The Harvard and Shirley Shakers

"ONE GENERATION PASSETH AWAY, and another generation cometh; but the earth abideth forever." These words of Ecclesiastes testify to the ephemeral nature of most things, including human life and the products of man's creativity. Nowhere is the transient state of mankind's earthly destiny better illustrated than in the story of the Shakers and their villages in the Central Massachusetts communities of Harvard and Shirley. Remnants of that story—though still discernible—are fading fast, even though the Shakers have been gone only a little more than half a century.

Unfortunately, the villages were abandoned before an appreciation of the Shakers had matured; consequently, land and structures were put to new uses. Some buildings were altered, others were razed; still others were gutted by fire, and some were simply allowed to deteriorate.

There has been a belated effort to restore Shaker sites elsewhere throughout the country, as nostalgia for the past begins to match America's preoccupation with the present and obsession with the future. But so far only minimal attention has been given to Harvard and Shirley, which played a central role in Shaker his-

1

tory, and which therefore merit memorializing, even if the commemoration consists only in retelling their story.

The Shakers were the most successful of the communistic societies of the nineteenth century, both in terms of their duration, geographic scope, membership and economic independence and in their impact as a model for other religious and social theorists. The Shaker experiment won the attention of such diverse individuals as Henry George, Friedrich Engels, Count Leo Tolstoy, and Alexis de Tocqueville.

In sheer numbers, Shaker communities exceeded other communitarian experiments, with a maximum of 6,000 members. This compared to an aggregate membership of 4,500 for all the Fourierist phalanxes. The Amana Community peaked at 1,800 and Robert Owen's New Harmony group had 900. George Rapp's Harmonists totalled 1,000; Icarians and Separatists each had 500; and both the Perfectionists at Oneida, New York, and the Ephratists in Pennsylvania numbered 300 members.

Historians seem to agree on two points: first, that the New World and, in particular, the new republic invited all sorts of social experimentation; and, secondly, that the most successful communitarian experiments were those—such as the Shakers—which were primarily motivated by a shared religious belief rather than merely a social conviction. That the Shakers survived longest of all may be due to the quality of their leadership.

Shakers originated in Manchester, England, in the mid-1700s, with the conversion of a poor, illiterate factory girl, Ann Lee, to a form of Quakerism later distinguished by Ann's celibate obsession. Ann had had four children, all of whom had died in infancy.

Mother Ann, as she came to be called because of her greater success as a spiritual mother, came to America with eight followers in 1774, on the eve of the American Revolution. She envisioned that her ministry would flower in the New World—and it did, but not until 1780, and then was under Mother Ann's direct supervision for only four years, for she died in 1784. During half the period of her public ministry in America, Mother Ann's mission was headquartered in Harvard and Shirley.

The Shakers were not at first communitarian. But because of persecution, the difficulty of making a living, and a belief in the reality of the Second Coming and the start of the millennium, the Shakers chose to gather in community.

Shaker villages were established in more than a dozen locations in New York and New England. Communities later took hold in Ohio, Kentucky, and Indiana during the period of the Second Awakening. Membership peaked in the mid-1800s; perhaps 20,000 persons were involved in the movement throughout its history.

As headquarters for the missionary travels of the first founders, Harvard and Shirley were important in the early years of the Shakers. It was in Harvard and Shirley that the most barbarous persecution of the Shakers took place—in large part because they were freshly arrived from England. Though the majority of Americans were of English descent, especially in New England, they had come to hate a monarchy that had since 1760 become more intolerable in its policies, and the Shakers' pacifism invited the same contempt accorded loyalists.

By the spring of 1781, when the Shakers came to Harvard from New York state, the Revolution was five years old. Cornwallis, in fact, surrendered at Yorktown on October 19 of that year, signaling the end of England's attempt to put down rebellion. But colonists remained hostile, and official peace did not come until two years later.

Once the ill feelings of the war had subsided, people regarded the Shakers with a more tolerant attitude. Certainly some aspects of Shaker religious expression were considered bizarre, but religious freedom, after all, was to be guaranteed in the Bill of Rights. Besides, there seems to have been quite a lot that was bizarre in those first experimental decades of the republic.

The Shakers taught that God was a dual personality, composed of a masculine spirit embodied in Christ and a female element manifested in the spiritual presence of Mother Ann. The way to spiritual perfection was best found in following a celibate life. The Shakers were not alone in advocating celibacy; many of the religious communitarian sects of the time shared similar beliefs.

The Rappites at Harmony and the Separatists of Zoar adopted celibacy early in their history, and so did Jemima Wilkinson, known as the Universal Friend. Wilkinson may have been influenced by the teaching of Mother Ann, and even her manner of death seems to have been patterned on that of Shadrack Ireland, Mother Ann's predecessor in Harvard. Both Ireland and Wilkinson boasted of physical immortality. At their deaths, the bodies of both were kept above ground awaiting resurrection before being walled up in cellars and then buried.

Millennialism was another common thread, many sects believing that the Second Coming had been achieved in the persons of their founders or that the millennium was imminent. The Shakers were pacifists, as were the Ephratists, among others; but though Shaker pacifism was a problem during the Revolution, the Ephratists' pacifism was respected. The Ephratists were German and had been well established in community long before the Revolution. They were able to render assistance to the sick and wounded of Washington's army.

Religious groups sometimes thrive because of persecution. This seems to have been the case in Harvard and Shirley, as believers flocked to hear the word of Mother Ann even as mob members abused them unmercifully. After Mother Ann's departure and her death a year later, her followers maintained themselves in a loose confederation until the next decade, when communities were officially gathered.

The Harvard community lasted from 1791 to 1918; Shirley, from 1793 to 1908. Each village accumulated about 2,000 acres of land. Harvard's Shaker population peaked at somewhat over 200; Shirley had about 150. The Harvard–Shirley bishopric served as a way station for travel and commerce between the Shaker communities in Northern New England and those in New York. Some of the Shakers' greatest inventions originated there, and Shaker music was governed for half a century by the notation system of a Shirley brother.

The Shakers were in their greatest glory during the first half of the nineteenth century. Their collective muscle and wit were joined in consecrated labor, with exemplary results in agriculture, animal husbandry, and handcrafts. But increasing industrialization introduced machinery and concepts which rendered Shaker arts obsolete. The idea of interchangeable parts paved the way for mass production and the assembly line; steam engines provided reliable power exceeding the brute strength of man and beast and eliminating reliance on wind and stream. Canals and railroads opened the nation to sophisticated commerce.

America had been a crucible for testing schemes that had previously been thought impossible—or been suppressed by Old World traditions—but even Americans were becoming bored with social experimenting. The public had been sated with countless -isms and -ologies in the 1840s: Millerism, Transcendentalism, Swedenborgianism, Fourierism, phrenology, mesmerism, hydropathy, and Grahamism were only some of these.

The old revivalists like Jonathan Edwards and George Whitefield had been succeeded by men like Charles Finney and Dwight Moody. But revivalism was on the decline, and a greater percentage of the public perceived an element of sleaziness in the new revivalists, precursors to the huckster.

The Civil War, finally, brought an end to the search for utopia. The public concentrated instead on the class struggles of the factory system and the new opportunities brought on by Western expansion. The Shakers were well on their way to becoming an anachronism.

After Mother Ann's death, Harvard and Shirley moved from the center stage of Shaker attention. New Lebanon, New York, as the seat of the Parent Ministry and central administration, was more important. Later, with the closing of communities, including New Lebanon, central administration shifted to the Shaker village at Hancock in western Massachusetts and then, upon Hancock's closing, to Canterbury, New Hampshire. Nowadays, Canterbury and the village at Sabbathday Lake in Maine can boast the distinction of having what would seem to be the last few Shakers in residence. Restoration work at other former villages, including those in the South, have sparked a resurgence of tourist interest.

However, Harvard and Shirley retain their historical identity as the stage upon which much of the Shaker drama was enacted.

This book once more directs the spotlight of attention to these communities. The leading character is Mother Ann; her personality permeates the history of Harvard and Shirley. The supporting cast is no less interesting; the Shakers whose stories are told here were memorable men and women. Above all, the villages of Harvard and Shirley, in their years of formation, prosperity, and decline, clearly demonstrate the Shaker philosophy and way of life. Shakerism was a living drama; the history of the Shaker communities of Harvard and Shirley bears witness to its unique identity.

2. From Lancashire to America

Because she was of humble parentage, the circumstances of Ann Lee's birth are obscure. Shaker sources say she was born "the last day of February" 1736 in Manchester, England. (This was a leap year; Shakers have celebrated her birth either on February 29 or March 1.) George II was then on the throne, and John Wesley was establishing the doctrine of Methodism; the Industrial Revolution was about to transform the economy of nations.

Charles Dickens gave this thinly veiled description of the industrial Manchester of succeeding decades in his novel *Hard Times*, as he portrayed the fictional community of Coketown:

"It was a town of red brick, or a brick that would have been red if the smoke and ashes had allowed it, but as matters stood it was a town of unnatural red and black like the painted face of a savage. It was a town of machinery and tall chimneys, out of which interminable serpents of smoke trailed themselves forever and ever, and never got uncoiled. It had a black canal in it, and a river that ran purple with ill-smelling dye, and vast piles of buildings full of windows where there was a rattling and a trembling all day long . . . . It contained several large streets all very like one another, inhabited by people equally like one another, who all went in and out at the same hours, with the same sound upon the same pavements, to do the same work, and to whom every day was the same as yesterday and tomorrow, and every year the counterpart of the last and the next."[1]

Manchester was the leading textile center and would have the distinction of becoming the mechanized prototype of the modern urban world, thanks to Richard Arkwright's invention of the first spinning frame and Samuel Crompton's development of the spinning mule. Working conditions were harsh; striking workmen would later smash the machines they blamed for their misery.

Six years after her birth, Ann's baptism is recorded in Manchester Cathedral in an entry dated June 1, 1742.[2] She was the second eldest of eight children of John Lee, a blacksmith. Though poor, he was "respectable in character, moral in principle, honest and punctual in his dealings, and industrious in business." The same Shaker source describes Ann Lee's mother as a "religious and very pious person."[3] She died while Ann was still young, probably as the result of childbirth.

Ann grew up on what was then known as Toad Lane, since renamed Todd Street. [4] The Lee children, like children in other poor families in that age, did not receive any formal education, but became part of the child labor force of the Industrial Revolution. During her youth Ann worked in a cotton factory, and was afterwards a cutter of hatter's fur. She was also, for some time, employed as a cook in the Manchester infirmary.

Long before Ann became a religious radical, the seeds of her celibate affinities were sown. A Shaker commentator would later relate: "It is remarkable that in early youth, she [Ann] had a great abhorrence of the fleshy cohabitation of the sexes, and so great was her sense of impurity, that she often admonished her mother against it, which, coming to her father's ears, he threatened, and actually attempted to whip her; upon which she threw herself into her mother's arms, and clung around her to escape his strokes."[5]

But fate—or perhaps her father—had not ordained a life of spinsterhood for Ann. Shaker sources tell us that "through the importunities of her relations" she was married to Abraham

Standerin (or Stanley), a blacksmith by trade.[6] She was wed on January 5, 1761, in Manchester Cathedral; both she and her husband, illiterate, signed the registry with crosses next to their names.

Though married in the Anglican church, Ann had already displayed religious individualism by joining a Quaker splinter group, under the leadership of James and Jane Wardley, four years before her marriage. She did not assume a leadership role in this society, however, until after experiencing personal tragedy.

Ann had four children, three of whom died in infancy; "One only, which was a daughter, attained to the age of about six years."[7] The last child died in October, 1766.

It is understandable that a woman with her bitter experiences might reject, even loathe, marital relations. Over the course of time, Ann's agony evolved into a religious revelation, and Ann took command of the Wardley group and made celibacy one of its most distinctive tenets.

Wardley followers met in Manchester, Bolton, and other localities in Lancashire. Tradition holds that they were inspired by the remnants of the Camisards, or French prophets, who fled France for English sanctuary in 1706. These prophets escaped Catholic-inspired royal persecution when the Edict of Nantes, which had granted religious liberty to the Protestants, was revoked in 1685. The Protestant peasantry of the Cevennes mountains in southern France who staged a bloody uprising in 1702 were Camisards. A Camisard leader was burned alive and others were broken on the wheel following savage attacks on Catholic churches. Those who fled to England—where the Glorious Revolution of 1689 seemed to fulfill a prophecy of the fall of Catholicism—gradually dwindled in influence, although there remained those who "like faithful watchmen of the night, waited the approaching dawn."[8]

Religious agitation marked the early eighteenth century. John Wesley was addressing the industrial proletariat with his Methodist commitment to the efficacy of faith. George Whitefield was launching a revival that attracted Englishmen and later ignited what was termed the Great Awakening in America. Ann Lee would later be quoted by her American followers as relating:

"When Whitefield first set out, he had great power and gifts of God. I was one of his hearers in England, but after he came to America he was persecuted for his testimony. He then returned to England, and took protection under the King; by which means he lost the power of God, and became formal, like other professors."[9]

The Shakers were influenced by the evangelism around them, of course. They also owe a debt to the Quakers, with whom they sometimes are confused. The Quakers had a reputation for radical behavior in the 1600s, as did the Shakers in the 1700s. Both groups emerged as staunch pacifists in their second century. Both groups deplored the influence of the Antichrist, a demoniac presence suggested by certain Biblical passages and personified by assorted enemies of the Redeemer throughout the centuries. In the Middle Ages, the church hurled the epithet of Antichrist at selected heretics. In return, dissidents, including the Shakers, saw Antichrist in the institution of the papacy itself. *Testimony of Christ's Second Appearing*—sometimes referred to as the Shaker Bible—is replete with denunciations of the Antichrist and refers to the established church of the Middle Ages as the "Mother of Harlots."[10]

Whatever theological reasoning guided Shakerism in its long history, the motive for Ann Lee's initial activism was prosaic. The deaths of her four children convinced her that she was being punished for her incontinence. Shaker source books record her sickness and anguish and quote her as saying:

"In my travail and tribulation, my sufferings were so great, that my flesh consumed upon my bones, and bloody sweat pressed through the pores of my skin." She went on this way for some nine years, and, while thus tormented, finally experienced a crucial revelation, the essence of her creed: "In these extraordinary manifestations, she had a full and clear view of the mystery of iniquity, of the root and foundation of human depravity and of the very act of transgression committed by the first man and the first woman, in the Garden of Eden. Here she saw whence and wherein all mankind were lost from God, and clearly realized the only possible way of recovery."[11] The vision so described occurred in prison during the summer of 1770.

Ann's confinement on this occasion represented only one of a series of encounters between the early Shakers and civil authorities. Court records depict the episodes as tawdry disturbances of the peace; Shaker sources portray them in heroic terms.

In one instance Ann and her father John—who had grown supportive of his daughter's religious attitudes—and three others were arrested on assault charges, and a claim was made for restitution to defray damages to the ironwork of a private dwelling. Ann and her father were sentenced to a month in prison. The next October, Ann's brother William was detained after a Shaker meeting adjourned in a brawl.

The Manchester *Mercury* carried this account: "Saturday last ended the Quarter Sessions, when John Townley, John Jackson, Betty Lees, and Ann Lees (Shakers) for going into Christ Church, in Manchester, and there willfully and contemptuously, in the time of the Divine service, disturbing the congregation then assembled at morning prayers in the said church, were severally fined £20 each."[12]

Ann must have been unable to pay her fine, and was sentenced to prison. The exact length of her sentence is not known, though various accounts indicate that several weeks is a likely guess.

Shaker sources give a different view: "A number of spies had been previously placed in the streets, under a pretense of preventing people from profaning the sabbath. The believers assembled that morning at the house of John Lee, and began their worship, as usual, by singing and dancing. This was discovered by the spies, and a mob was soon raised, headed by the principal warden, who surrounded the house, burst open the doors, and ascended the stairs into the third loft, where the believers were assembled. They were all seized without any ceremony, and immediately dragged down stairs; Mother Ann herself was dragged down by her feet and very much abused. They were all, excepting one man and two children, immediately hurried off to the stone prison, and put into close confinement. The next morning they were all released excepting Mother Ann and John Lee, her father, who were removed to the house of correction, where they were kept confined several weeks, and then discharged."[13]

On one occasion, some type of spiritual force-field was credited in saving Ann from being stoned by an angry mob. Another
favorite anecdote relates that Ann was placed in solitary confinement without food or drink for two weeks—long enough to cause
her death. However, James Whittaker, a youthful follower,
gained access to the prison cell and fed Ann by inserting the stem
of a tobacco pipe into the keyhole of the cell door, then pouring
quantities of liquid into the bowl. It is said her jailers were aston-
ished when her confinement ended and she emerged as healthy as
the day she entered.[14] (Historian Edward Deming Andrews dis-
counts this story as a fable, asserting that "prisoners were not
starved to death for breaking the Sabbath. Furthermore, in the
Manchester house of correction the inmates were kept on the second floor, where there would be no keyhole accessible to the
street."[15])

The incident of Ann's deliverance from prison, in any event,
was seen by the Wardley group as evidence of Ann's favored position. She related her spiritual visions and revealed herself as Ann
the Word. She was subsequently called Mother Ann.

Apart from the supernatural qualities sometimes ascribed to
Mother Ann, there seems little doubt that she possessed great personal magnetism. She became the acknowledged leader of the
Shaker group in Manchester, even though the group included
members of superior social status. Two of these were John Hocknell, described as a person with considerable property, and his
brother-in-law, John Townley.[16] Townley aided the believers during the Wardley period. Mother Ann also managed to attract her
father to her cause (despite earlier differences with him), and also
her brother, William, a one-time soldier renowned for his physical
strength and by his own admission "a proud, haughty young man,
fond of dress and gaiety" before he realized his sinful ways.[17]
Mother Ann even secured the tenuous allegiance of her husband,
though their marriage had become celibate. Most impressive of
all, she eventually attracted gifted clergymen.

Mother Ann guided the Shaker sect in England for four years.
She then—in 1774—"by special revelation, was directed to repair

to America; and at the same time, she received a divine promise, that the work of God would greatly increase, and the millennial church would be established in that country."[18]

Moved to action by this revelation, Mother Ann and a group of her followers arranged to emigrate. The group included her husband, Abraham Stanley, her brother, William Lee, her niece, Nancy Lee, John Hocknell and his son, Richard Hocknell, James Shepherd (one of those who witnessed Ann's marriage banns), Mary Partington (at whose home some of the worship services were held), and James Whittaker.

Hocknell arranged for passage aboard the ship *Mariah* under the command of a Captain Smith of New York. The group journeyed from Manchester to the dock city of Liverpool, where they set out into the Irish Sea on May 10, leaving relatives and the remainder of the Wardley group behind.

Tradition has it that the captain became annoyed in midvoyage with his passengers' antics, which included dancing on deck and singing hymns. He threatened to have them thrown overboard. But providence intervened, according to Shaker sources, when heavy seas loosened a plank and caused the vessel to leak badly. The captain was in despair, but Mother Ann assured him: "Captain, be of good cheer; there shall not a hair of our heads perish, we shall all arrive safe to America. I just now saw two bright angels of God standing by the mast, through whom I received this promise."[19]

Shortly thereafter, a large wave struck the ship with great violence and the loose plank was restored in place. Thereafter, the captain allowed the Shakers to worship in their own fashion.

The *Mariah* survived the nearly three-month-long Atlantic crossing and arrived in New York Harbor on August 6, 1774. The Shakers immediately split up, most going to the Albany area. John Hocknell soon returned to England to get the rest of his family. Mother Ann and her husband took up residence in a house in New York City on Queen Street—later renamed Pearl Street—with a family by the name of Cunningham. Abraham secured employment as a blacksmith in the family business; Ann became a domestic in the household.

The record of Abraham Stanley's relationship with his wife is sketchy. Mother Ann once said of him, "The man to whom I was married . . . would have been willing to pass through a flaming fire for my sake if I would but live in the flesh with him, which I refused to do."[20] Others describe him as being a lukewarm Shaker. "Though he never had been considered as a faithful and substantial believer; yet he had hitherto supported his credit and reputation and maintained an outward conformity to his faith."[21]

But now a crisis developed, and the thirteen-year-old marriage unraveled. Abraham became seriously ill, and Mother Ann nursed him back to health. Once again able to walk the streets, he took to carousing and finally brought a "lewd" woman home with him, demanding that his wife agree to cohabit with him or else he would abandon her. Ann entreated him to renounce "this wickedness" and return to the faith, and berated him for repaying her kindness with such behavior. But Abraham was adamant. He left Mother Ann, took up with his female companion, moved to a distant part of the city and severed his connection with his former life.

Meanwhile, John Hocknell returned from England accompanied by his family and with funds to secure a parcel of wilderness property at Niskayuna, seven miles northwest of Albany. Mother Ann and the other Shakers were reunited, and the group established a settlement in the summer of 1776. They were determined to clear the forested and swampy area and grow crops; this endeavor occupied them for more than three years.

Eighteenth century New Englanders were accustomed to bizarre displays of the spirit. Since the time of the Great Awakening of the 1740s, when Jonathan Edwards and the Grand Itinerants—George Whitefield, Gilbert Tennent, and James Davenport—addressed the multitudes, there were frequent outpourings of the spirit. The revivalists were regarded as divine instruments. Those who supported their message were called New Lights.

Revivalist sermons attracted hordes of listeners; Whitefield, for instance, attracted an estimated twenty to thirty thousand listeners at the Boston Common.[22] The people were attuned to extreme oratory, which accounts for the popularity of such speakers as James Davenport, regarded as the arch-fanatic of the Great Awakening.

About this time a New Light Baptist revival erupted at the Berkshire border of New York and Massachusetts. The revival flourished principally in New Lebanon, New York, and in Hancock, Massachusetts, under the leadership of Joseph Meacham, a lay preacher from Enfield, Connecticut, and the Reverend Samuel Johnson, former Presbyterian minister at New Lebanon. The fervor of the revival subsided in the fall of 1779, but was reignited the next year when travelers happened on the Niskayuna settlement and discovered the doctrine of a realized Second Coming.

Joseph Meacham sent an envoy to challenge Mother Ann's dominant role of religious leadership.

"Saint Paul says," the envoy inquired, "let your women keep silence in the Churches; for it is not permitted unto them to speak; but they are commanded to be under obedience as also saith the law. And if they will learn anything, let them ask their husbands at home; for it is a shame for a woman to speak in the Church. But you not only speak, but seem to be an Elder in your Church. How do you reconcile this with the Apostle's doctrine?"

Mother Ann responded with a parable comparing the authority to speak in religious matters to the hierarchy of authority existing in the natural family: "The man is the first, and the woman the second in the government of the family. He is the father and she the mother; and all the children, both male and female, must be subject to the parents; and the woman being second, must be subject to her husband, who is the first; but when the man is gone, the right of government belongs to the woman: So is the family of Christ."[23]

Mother Ann's position accommodated nicely the prevailing attitude toward the female. However, such emotions remained an element in resentment toward the sect; and this was not the only source of friction. With the American Revolution at its height and distrust of Tories running high, patriots saw in the English ancestry of the Shakers, coupled with their recent arrival and policy of nonresistance, more than a suspicion of pro-British sentiment.

Nevertheless, the sect grew rapidly. Persons from throughout New York and New England visited Mother Ann. Returning to their homes, they established a network of believers who would soon become the nucleus of communal societies.

Mother Ann found fertile ground for her teaching after the New Lebanon revival. New Light Baptists channeled freshly charged spiritual energies into the service of Shaker doctrine. As people began seeking the Shakers out in greater numbers, the elders cast about for converts in places where other revivalist activity had taken hold. Those who wondered what to do with their reborn lives flocked to the Shakers, answering the call to confess their sins and divest themselves of their fleshly ways.

The message of Mother Ann may also have been enhanced by meteorological coincidence. Legend refers to Joseph Meacham's meeting with Mother Ann on the famous (and historically documented[24]) "dark day" of May 10, 1780. "Though there were neither clouds nor smoke in the atmosphere, the sun did not appear all that day through parts of New England, and people were out wringing their hands and howling, 'The Day of Judgment is come.'"[25] This was the day of the first public opening of the testimony of Niskayuna, so Shaker tradition records.)

Mother Ann's appearance was conspicuous and her personality magnetic. She was a woman in her mid-forties as she opened her testimony in America and is described as being "rather below the common stature of woman; thick set, but straight and otherwise well proportioned and regular in form and features. Her complexion," Shaker contemporaries noted, "was light and fair, and her eyes were blue, but keen and penetrating; her countenance was mild and expressive, but grave and solemn. Her natural constitution was sound, strong and healthy. Her manners were plain, simple and easy; yet she possessed a certain dignity of appearance that inspired confidence and commanded respect. By many of the world, who saw her without prejudice," the Shakers said, "she was called beautiful; and to her faithful children, she appeared to possess a degree of dignified beauty and heavenly love, which they had never before discovered among mortals."[26]

History has had to rely on this word picture of Mother Ann; her life predated photography, and early Shaker doctrine banned portraits and other forms of painting as superfluous.

An early convert, Richard Treat, reported, "Many times have I seen her on her knees, with the tears flowing from her eyes and dropping on the floor, crying to God with such cries as I never before heard from any mortal. . . . At other times she was filled with great joy, and would fill a whole assembly with joy in a few minutes. Even the heavenly joy that seemed to shine in her countenance, was sufficient to cheer the heart of every beholder."[27]

There are also a number of references to Mother Ann's supposed clairvoyant abilities. One believer, Prudence Hammond, told of meeting Mother Ann for the first time, whereupon Ann "told me of some circumstances, and mentioned a number of transactions of my childhood and youth, which I knew it impossible for her to know but by divine inspiration."[28] Prudence further reported that her hearing was restored; this was just one of several testimonials by the faithful of Ann's healing power.[29]

Mother Ann also had the good fortune that the populace around New Lebanon and Hancock had convinced themselves to expect the second coming of Christ. Those awaiting a redeemer in the flesh included trained clergymen as well as the unlettered. The Reverend Samuel Johnson, for instance, who graduated from Yale as a theology student, disputed the validity of traditional religion because he could not perceive in the established church evidence of the continuous succession of Christ. Johnson said he consulted the best divines of the day and learned that the Second Coming was near at hand.[30]

That the new arrival of the spirit should come in the form of a woman was a surprise—but not one that couldn't be accommodated. A follower, Anne Mathewson, said afterwards, "There are few in this day, who will pretend to deny the agency of the first woman in leading mankind into sin. Why should it be thought incredible that the agency of a woman should necessarily be first in leading the human race out of sin?"[31]

Apart from the messianic pretensions Mother Ann assumed for herself or that her followers ascribed to her, the Shaker belief was not unlike that of other denominations and sects of the time—except for the doctrine of celibacy, which implied that wrongs of the world could all be laid at the doorstep of carnal indulgence.

Daniel Moseley—yet another of the believers whose first person testimonials were gathered together for publication in the early decades of Shakerism—related that Mother Ann "exposed the subtle craftiness of that filthy nature in the males, by which they seek to seduce and debauch the females; and all the enticing arts of the females to ensnare and bewitch the males, and draw them into their wanton embraces."[32]

Moseley cataloged all the miseries that lust produces: deceit, hypocrisy, fraud, knavery, covetousness, injustice, theft, robbery, dissipation, idleness, contention, strife, hatred, envy, jealousy and murder among individuals, and war and bloodshed, destruction and rapine among nations. He quoted Mother Ann as saying, "These things are the fruits of the filthy gratifications of the flesh, which bring distress and poverty, shame and disgrace upon families and individuals, and fill the earth with wretchedness and misery."[33]

It made sense to many that celibacy had to be part of salvation. As Amos Stower, another believer, testified, "I sensibly felt the inconsistency of a person's pretending to be born of the Spirit, while living in the gratification of the desires and of the mind."[34]

New Englanders still labored with a puritan conscience, one which did not forbid sex but certainly frowned on its illicit enjoyment. The penalties for incontinence were often severe: public condemnation, scandalous pregnancy and the stain of illegitimacy, and frequently incurable venereal disease. Deformed creatures and imbeciles were only too visible as society, lacking asylums, was forced to allow these victims of God's wrath to mingle with the general populace.

Although the Shakers were taught to despise the carnal life, there was a measure of tolerance for those who yielded to temptation within the married state. Daniel Moseley quoted Mother Ann as telling him that he should not go and report that the Shakers forbid to marry: "For we do not," she said. "But all that cannot or will not take up their crosses for the Kingdom of Christ's sake, and that only, I would advise them to marry and live after the flesh, in a lawful manner, and be servants to their families—for that is natural," she said, "and less sinful in the sight of God than any other way of gratifying that nature."[35]

In 1780, Mother Ann was imprisoned, on a charge of treason, and kept in jail for half a year at Albany and then Poughkeepsie, New York. Her followers, however, managed to convince Governor George Clinton of her innocence, and she was released.

Mother Ann's incarceration only served to enhance her fame. It was decided that the time had come to embark on a missionary visit to the home communities of converts throughout New England.

On May 31, 1781, a group composed of Mother Ann, William Lee and James Whittaker, Samuel Fitch, Mary Partington, Margaret Leeland, John Farington, and James Shepherd set out on a journey to Harvard, Massachusetts. The journey there and back was to last two years and three months, with stops in Massachusetts, Connecticut, and New York.[36] In addition, delegations from Maine and New Hampshire visited Mother Ann at her missionary headquarters in Harvard. The seed would thereby be planted for the New England communities which the Shakers would organize in the next decade.

3. Harvard and Shirley

Harvard's rural countenance was placid. In the center of town, cottages surrounded a spacious common at the foot of Pin Hill. The open space served as training ground for the militia; two companies had marched the dozen miles or so to join other minutemen in the fighting at Concord.[1] A burial ground was set apart at one end of the common. The half-century-old Congregational meeting house stood sentinel over citizen morals and provided a forum for public debate. In the Still River section, a Baptist meeting house had recently been erected to rival the edifice in the center. Elsewhere, farms and orchards, gristmills and sawmills, cottage industries, and small family holdings were sparsely distributed over Harvard's hills and valleys.

The Shakers were interested in a secluded hollow in the northeast section of town which had been the domain of Shadrack Ireland. The death of this cult leader a year earlier had left about a dozen followers, who lived at or near the so-called Square House, which took its name from its nearly flat roof.

Little is known about Ireland's early life. He came from the Boston harbor community of Charlestown, and was a pipemaker, according to Charlestown records, a joiner or carver in other accounts.[2] Inspired by the evangelism of George Whitefield, Ireland became a New Light preacher. One day he left his radical ministry in Charlestown, deserted his wife and six children, and fled to Harvard. Ireland preached that he had been "called of the Lord to forsake wife and family."[3] Nevertheless, he took a soul mate, Abigail Lougee, as his spiritual bride.

Ireland found in Harvard enough separatist dissidents to constitute a following. In 1769, he presided over the building of the Square House. His helpers included Isaac Willard, who once had lived in Charlestown and may have suggested the Harvard refuge to Ireland,[4] Zaccheus Stephens, David Hoar, Abel Jewett, Samuel and Jonathan Cooper, Ethan Phillips and John Manor.[5] There was a secret passageway running from the cellar to a rooftop cupola. Here Ireland kept a lookout, fearing either that his abandoned family would catch up with him or that civil authorities would prosecute him for blasphemy. Ireland had charged that the Congregational clergy were sunk in sloth and self-indulgence.[6]

Ireland fancied himself fortified with the Biblical Bread of Life, claimed he was immortal, and warned his subjects not to bury him if he appeared to die. He told them he planned to rise again, either on the third day or on the ninth. In due course—in the summer of 1780—Ireland died. An old Shaker manuscript records the circumstances:

"The night he died he walked the floor in great distress of mind and groaning with deep groans. He said, 'I feel the wrath of God' . . . Abigail Lougee called Abigail Cooper to get up and light a light. They got a light as quick as they could, but he was gone when they got to him."[7]

It was several days before Ireland's followers relegated his decomposing remains to the cellar. After several weeks, the foul presence was taken off to a cornfield at night. The task of burying the corpse fell to Abijah Worster and David Hoar. They uprooted five hills of corn and dug a grave for their all too mortal leader, replanted the corn, and left the grave unmarked.[8]

For a time, David Hoar took over as leader, assisted by *his* spiritual helper, Malabar Bean, who is described as "a designing

woman."[9] At some point, members of the Ireland group are believed to have heard about the teachings of Mother Ann Lee. Like
Ireland, she advocated communal sharing and nonresistance.
Zaccheus Stephens probably visited Niskayuna and invited
Mother Ann to visit the Ireland enclave in Harvard. (Mother Ann
had often spoken to her followers of a place in America that she
had seen in vision while in England. Whether it was this vision or
Stephens's invitation that suggested Harvard as her missionary
destination is not known, but Shaker historians specifically refer to
her setting out "on a journey to Harvard."[10])

Mother Ann spent her first night in Harvard at Stephens's
house and then stayed a week at the Willards'. Isaac Willard was a
man in his early sixties who in his youth had served as a soldier in
the French War. His reputation for religious nonconformity began
thirty years before Mother Ann's coming, when he, his wife, and
two other couples raised a row of some sort in the Congregational
meeting house. Long before he joined Ireland, he was described as
"peculiar in his religious views and indulging in distempered
fancies."[11]

In a vision, while staying at Isaac Willard's, Mother Ann saw
a large mob, in black, which filled the road leading to the Square
House, and which seemed opposed to her going there. She then
saw two angels, who made their way through the mob, by which
she perceived that God would open the way for her to go.[12]

Encouraged by this vision, Mother Ann set off from the
Willard home, accompanied by her party, and approached the
Square House. Abigail Cooper, who had been present on the night
of Ireland's death, lived there with her family and other former
Ireland adherents.

Father William Lee asked her, "Are you willing we should
come into your house?"

Abigail replied, "No, I don't know as I am."

But when Father William pressed to be granted admission,
Abigail relented.

"I suppose I must," she said.[13]

The visitors were no sooner inside than they asked Abigail if
she were satisfied with her religion. Abigail responded that she

had seen a great deal of false religion and did not want to see any more. Further, if they had any new religion, they could keep it to themselves, she did not want it, nor did she care about seeing them.

"I have seen you before," said Mother Ann, looking at Abigail. Then, looking around on others who occupied the dwelling, she continued, "And so I have seen you all."

The Shakers left shortly to visit the home of John Cooper, about a mile north of the Square House. Upon leaving they asked Abigail if she loved them. She did not, she said; but Father William gave her an apple and told Abigail they would make her love them.

Sure enough, as Abigail was later to testify, she was won over. She took the apple that Father William offered and placed it on the mantlepiece.

"They had not been gone long," she afterwards confided, "before I could say in truth that I did love them. I loved the apple they gave me, for their sakes. When I was about my work I would now and then look at the apple, and take it in my hand. I knew they had something good about them because I loved them. So I wanted they should come back, and when they came I was thankful to take them in, and glad to do anything for them I could do."[14]

Mother Ann soon won the devotion of most of Ireland's followers. David Hoar was an exception. Disgruntled by his displacement as the new leader, Hoar is said to have alerted Ireland's heirs in Charlestown. The legal heirs consisted of Jonathan Ireland, a blacksmith in Salem, his wife, Elizabeth, Martha Davis, and Thomas and Tabitha Robbins of Charlestown. The heirs acquired title and offered to sell the property to its occupants. Mother Ann instructed Aaron Jewett, a Littleton believer, to negotiate the purchase, the price being £500.[15]

Although Mother Ann quickly made the remnants of Ireland's group her own, she mocked Ireland's delusion and reminded the mostly elderly flock of their mortality.

"You are old people," she told them, "yet you think you shall never die! One is dropping away here, and another there, amongst you; yet you lay it to some secret cause—to something which they have done. That is to say, if they had been faithful, it would not have been so. Look at yourselves; you carry about you all the marks of mortality that are on other people. Your skins are wrinkled; your hair is turning white and falling from your heads; your eyesight is failing; you are losing your teeth, and your bodies are growing decrepit. How inconsistent it is for you to think you shall never die! These natural bodies must all die and turn to dust."[16]

Mother Ann took pains to discredit Ireland even beyond his belated grave, making disparaging references to Ireland's spirit, with which she claimed to commune. Once she told her followers, "Shadrack Ireland has been here to see me; and I made labors with him, but he would not believe; therefore he was left to feel hell, and souls in that state were frightened at him, because his sufferings were so much greater than theirs. But he will never be released, until some of his people find their redemption."[17] (Mother Ann's entreaties with Ireland's spirit were consistent with the Shaker view that salvation was still possible beyond the grave.)

About a month after the Shakers arrived in town, a report circulated that the Shakers had come there with seventy wagons and 600 stands of arms. One David Whitney of the town asserted that "a certain man" had told him that he had seen a curious chest of firearms at the Square House.

Other disparaging accounts of Shaker activities also began appearing. The first such piece was written by apostate Valentine Rathbun and described a meeting in Harvard:

"They meet together in the night, and have been heard two miles by the people in the dead of night; sometimes a company of them will run away to some house, get into it, raise up a bedlam, wake up all in the house, and the neighbors round about for a mile. They run about in the woods and elsewhere hooting and tooting like owls. . . ."[18]

Another apostate, Amos Taylor, a native of Groton, followed an erratic career as teacher, poet, publisher, and bookseller. His brother Ephraim was a member of the Harvard Shakers for a number of years. Taylor described meetings held at the Square House "every night until about two o'clock after midnight, and very frequently until the break of day,"[19] with much wild leaping about, yelling, singing and rolling on the floor.

These descriptions by persons one would expect to be hostile tally closely with a slightly later one by an impartial observer, William Plumer, who eventually became governor of New Hampshire and a United States senator. Plumer visited Harvard in 1782 as an aspiring attorney in his early twenties. After attending a Harvard service one evening, he described Shaker conduct as being "so wild and extravagant that it was some time before I could believe my own senses." Their services continued, he said, until many of the participants were shaking and trembling. "The motion proceeded from the heads to the hands, arms and whole body, with such power as if limb would rend from limb."

Plumer observed a young Shaker who whirled about for nearly an hour. It was not a voluntary motion, she said when he asked her about this, but was caused by a supernatural impulse.

"I asked," Plumer wrote, "whether a man could, by his strength, prevent her shaking and whirling. She said it would be blasphemy against God to attempt such a thing. Some time after this, when she was whirling with great velocity, I rose and advanced gradually towards her, clasped her in my arms, and in the course of a moment held her still, though she exclaimed against me as very rude and indecent."[20]

With such reports circulating, the Shakers immediately had to contend with the opposition of area clergymen. Reverend Moses Adams of Acton gave the Marlborough Association—a regional group of ministers—"an account of the strange conduct and temper of a number of people who were come to Harvard who were called Shakers, and under the guidance of 'an elect lady.'"

The town of Harvard decided to take action. On the town meeting warrant the following article appeared: "To hear and consider a petition of a number of inhabitants of Harvard and see if the town will, agreeable to said petition, consult and determine on some means to remove the people called Shaking Quakers who are collected together in this town."[21]

A committee was appointed, led by one Asa Houghton, to inquire into the matter. They went to the Square House, accompanied by the town militia captained by Ephraim Davis and supplemented by militiamen of surrounding towns. The Shakers were informed of the allegations against them. Elder James Whittaker asked to be permitted to speak to the assembly.

"I understand that you have heard that we have weapons of war here," he said, "and are apprehensive that we are enemies of the country; we are harmless, inoffensive people; we do not want to injure any man either in person or property; we want no man's silver nor gold, but only their souls to God; this is all we want of anyone; but if you believe those reports, you may have free liberty to search the house, or barn, or any of these surrounding buildings."

Father James's remarks mollified the less belligerent members of the delegation. Nevertheless, though the Shakers appeared harmless, Asa Houghton as head of the committee issued an ultimatum that the Shakers leave town. But Elder Whittaker was undaunted.

"We came here peaceably, and we can say, as was said of St. Paul, we dwell in our own hired house," said Whittaker.[22]

The confrontation continued till the latter part of the afternoon, when most of the delegation dispersed. Those who remained into the evening said they were curious to hear about Shaker beliefs. Accordingly, Father James addressed the company on the necessity of confessing their sins and reforming. Despite some heckling, the speech was well received; and some of the men even adopted the Shaker testimony.

Mother Ann and the leaders remained in Harvard during the fall and early winter. Somehow, enough provisions were maintained to accommodate everyone who came. But Mother Ann did not believe in relying solely on Providence.

Calling her follower Jonathan Slosson to her room one day, she compared their good fortune with that of the miracle of the loaves and fishes but warned that such could not always be so. She asked him if he knew of a way to obtain more bread for the multitude. Jonathan suggested that he journey to the communities of Lebanon, Hancock, and Richmond, more than one hundred miles away, where there was food in abundance. Mother Ann agreed and dispatched Jonathan and a companion, Reuben Harrison.

The men soon returned with supplies of flour and cheese. Mother Ann and the others wept and gave thanks for the generosity of their fellow believers.

In December, Mother Ann's party left the Square House for Petersham. Though Mother Ann was successful there among her flock, she was abducted one day by ruffians who began to disrobe her, ostensibly to determine whether she were actually a woman or a man in disguise. Male Shakers rescued her, and the harried group returned to Harvard in January, 1782.

Later that month, a body of militia led by Captain Phineas Farnworth descended on the Square House, intending to drive off the Shakers. With clubs on their shoulders, they surrounded the building. Mother Ann told Captain Farnworth that she expected to be gone the following morning, if it were God's will. Satisfied, Farnworth agreed not to bother the worshippers further, even when Mother Ann qualified her willingness to leave by asserting, "I expect to go tomorrow, but I will return the next day, if it is God's will, for all you."[17]

The next day Mother Ann did leave, for a short time; but her return was also brief and apparently intended only to bolster the spirits of her followers. That night she went to Zaccheus Stephens's house, and the next day she departed for towns in Connecticut and western Massachusetts.

Meanwhile, a mob returned to the Square House, found Mother Ann missing, and became angry. A group went to Isaac Willard's house, where Elizur Goodrich and Lucy Wright, two Shaker leaders, were hiding, but left when Willard ordered the delegation off his property.

Mother Ann was gone from Harvard for the rest of the winter, spending two months in Ashfield. She returned with the elders to Harvard about the twentieth of May.

During the latter part of July, notice was circulated through the area towns calling for a meeting to be assembled at Harvard Common in preparation for driving the Shakers out of town. Shaker historians derisively claimed that Phineas Fairbank, a deacon of the First Congregational Church, contributed two barrels of cider "in order to stimulate the zeal" of the crowd. However,

the day in question was also the occasion of a ministers' meeting in
Harvard, and the ministers prevailed upon the crowd to restrain
themselves until the clergymen could speak with the Shakers. A
committee of four ministers, headed by Zabdiel Adams—so-called
Bishop of Lunenburg and a double cousin of patriot John
Adams[24]—set off for the Square House.

Adams informed the Shakers of the suspicions of the townspeople and inquired if they were friends of America and if they
would fight for the American cause.

Mother Ann, James Whittaker and Aaron Jewett, the latter a
former Revolutionary War officer, confronted the ministers.
Whittaker, as the chief spokesman, said the Shakers were friends
to the souls of all men, but would not engage in killing.

"But," he added, "we will fight your enemy and the enemy of
all mankind, that is, the devil."[25]

The Reverend Mr. Adams quizzed Whittaker regarding
Shaker attitudes toward marriage. Jesus Christ did not disapprove
of marriage, he pointed out, and had in fact contributed to the
marriage at Cana, turning water into wine for the guests to drink.
Whittaker replied that Christ's enemies had used the same argu-
ments to prove Christ a gluttonous man and a winebibber. He insisted that Jesus' attendance at the wedding proved an endorse-
ment neither of marriage nor of drunkenness.

Adams asked Mother Ann if the doctrine of celibacy were not
a threat to society, in view of property considerations and ques-
tions of inheritance. Mother Ann replied that she considered matrimony to be a civil custom, appropriate for the common men of
the world.

"But it does not, however, belong to Christ's true followers,"
she explained. "For that reason we have nothing to do with it.

"Paul taught the Corinthians," she continued, "that it was
better to marry than to burn and we have always so agreed. We
admit that marriage is useful in its place since it prevents many
evils. For the men of the world today, it is in fact absolutely necessary. Without it, the excesses of lust would destroy society and ruin
the human race. Of that, sirs, I am well aware. I will even admit
that marriage is honorable where people enter into it from conscientious motives. But I also contend that its frequent shameful

abuses are disgraceful and blot the custom of marriage itself."[26]

Adams seemed satisfied, and he bade the Shakers farewell with a friendly warning concerning the intentions of the group assembled at the town common. He advised Mother Ann for her own good to leave the vicinity.

Returning to Harvard center, the clergymen instructed the gathering to disperse. The Reverend Mr. Adams was asked by one of the other ministers what he thought of the Shakers.

"I think the people better let them alone," Adams replied. "That Whittaker is a sharp man."[27]

Though the crisis of the moment had passed, the townspeople were not of a mind to leave the Shakers alone. Hostility intensified as more Shakers began arriving. Believers, having harvested their grain, came from New Lebanon, Hancock and other places in almost a holiday mood. These people assembled in the area of the Square House.

Mother Ann reported seeing a new vision of a mob and of being told by God to withdraw from Harvard. Forewarned, Mother Ann, William Lee and James Whittaker left Harvard, journeying first to Abel Jewett's house in Littleton and then to Nathan Kandal's in Woburn. Elder Hocknell was left in charge.

Mother Ann had departed on a Friday, August 16, 1782. The following Sunday, believers in great numbers attended Sabbath services at the Square House. Their zeal took the form of "singing, dancing, leaping, shouting, clapping of hands, and such other exercises as they were led into by the spirit," according to Shaker accounts. "But," Shaker sources said, "the sound of this meeting, though joyful to the believers, was terrible to the wicked; for the sound thereof was heard at the distance of several miles."[28]

Reaction was swift and violent. A crowd of irate citizens from Harvard and area towns marched upon the Square House. The Sabbath meeting lasted all day and into the evening. When the meeting adjourned, many of the believers went with neighboring Shakers to their homes to spend the night, but a large number remained in the Square House.

A gathering mob, which had grown to an estimated four hundred strong, began surrounding the Square House at dark. Those inside naturally became alarmed by the noise, and an aged brother opened a door to look out. Mob members pushed inside and made a search for Mother Ann, becoming infuriated when they discovered her missing.

Lucy Wright—later to be known as Mother Lucy—was present on that occasion, having come from Pittsfield. She tried to dissuade the interlopers from committing violence, but they threatened to push her down a flight of stairs. Realizing the danger, she and Mary Partington took pails, and, moving outside through the mob, walked to the barn as if they were intending to milk cows. After reaching the barn, they fled across a field.

They eventually reached safety at the home of Solomon Cooper, and word was spread of impending trouble at the Square House. The believers from the neighborhood converged on the Square House, shouldering their way through the sullen crowd into the house. With the Square House full to overflowing and with an estimated four hundred cudgel- and whip-carrying tormentors outside, Elder Hocknell called upon the assembly to kneel and beseech God's blessing.

Their devout display, however, served only to ignite the passions of the mob. Irate mob leaders forced the doors and barged inside. Shakers were seized by the throat, hair, and limbs and were roughly hauled outside. In the commotion, Elder Hocknell managed to separate himself from the scuffle by leaping over a fence and hiding in a garden area. Shaker sources contend that suddenly the power of God seized Hocknell and stretched out his hand to the east. "He immediately followed in that direction, which led him to Mother Ann, and he informed her of these things."[29] Mother Ann was in Woburn at the time, a community northwest of Boston and more than twenty miles east of Harvard.

Meanwhile the leaders of the mob—Phineas Farnworth, militia captain; Jonathan Pollard, lieutenant; Isaiah Whitney, Jonathan Houghton, and Asa Houghton—instructed the local believers to return to their homes. Those not of Harvard were given one hour to eat and prepare to get out of town. No protests were tolerated.

Once the hour had elapsed, the order was given to march and the sorry procession began. Resident Shakers stubbornly persisted in marching with the visiting brethren. Members of the mob were on horseback. Only Shaker women were permitted to ride. The mob quickened the pace of the marchers with liberal use of whips and cudgels.

The procession had gone only a short distance when Dyer Fitch received a beating about the face and head from Isaiah Whitney, who objected to Fitch's praying aloud. A short distance farther, Abijah Worster, who had just joined the marchers, was knocked over the head with a staff wielded by Asa Houghton. Worster had made the mistake of embracing James Shepherd in welcome.

Three miles farther on, the procession halted near Still River for "a little diversion." The order was given to whip Shepherd, the only original English Shaker in the company. Switches from bushes nearby were distributed. Shepherd was ordered to strip to the waist, and, as he took off his coat and jacket, he said to the brethren, "Be of good cheer; for it is your Heavenly Father's good pleasure to give you the Kingdom."[30]

As Shepherd's reward for this profession of faith, Isaiah Whitney administered several lashes with his horsewhip. Eleazer Rand leaped on Shepherd's back to protect him. The incensed mob proceeded to flail away at both of them.

A Bolton man named Priest seized Rand, beat him, and hurled him against a stone wall in a vain attempt to silence outcries of prayer. Another Shaker, William Morey, protested, but Captain Farnworth punched him in the face with such force that he knocked out several teeth. Morey, with blood streaming from his mouth, continued to protest.

The march continued to the Harvard–Bolton border, a distance of about six miles from the Square House. Some Harvard residents along the way disapproved of the actions of their fellow townspeople, but the temper of the mob did not yield to reason. The Harvard brethren tagged along to assist the distant believers, although warned not to do so. Eleazer Rand was struck by a club, suffering a broken arm.

The mob herded captives another seven miles through the town of Bolton to Lancaster; the whole journey was a nightmare of whipping, beating and clubbing. Shakers were pushed off bridges into the water and mud. Aged Shakers trying to gain some relief by mounting their horses were savagely beaten. One old man was slammed across the back with a fence rail.

Upon reaching Lancaster, the mob leaders told the nonresident believers never to return to Harvard or they would be whipped without benefit of judge or jury. In one last display of fury, the mob rode their horses among the believers, knocking several down and beating them as they attempted to kneel and thank the Almighty that they had been deemed worthy to suffer persecution for the spread of the Gospel. Afterwards, the Shakers continued their journey, receiving one last whipping from a man who blocked the road as they departed.

The Harvard Shakers turned back with the mob, and more cruelty was meted out. When the assembly reached Harvard again, it was decided that Abijah Worster should be whipped for "going about breaking up churches and families."[31] Twenty lashes were to be administered as Abijah stood tied to a tree at the Captain Thaddeus Pollard house. Jonathan Houghton laid on the first ten strokes, but the infamous sport was interrupted when a respected member of the community, James Haskell, rode by and rebuked the mob. Haskell tore off his coat and shrieked, "Here, here, if there are any more stripes to be taken let me take the rest."[32]

Haskell's moral influence was such that the mob abandoned their maliciousness and drifted away. Abijah was released and walked off singing, so the story goes.

The day had been a shameful one for the town of Harvard and for mob participants from the community and adjoining towns. The Shakers ever after maintained that a curse had befallen the perpetrators, and it was said that the "Shaker drivers" experienced various calamities in later life.[33]

But the persecution of that day did not suppress the fervor of the Shakers; in fact, the reverse seemed true. Shaker zeal, instead of abating, seemed to increase. Nor did the danger of mob violence deter Mother Ann from returning to Harvard.

Mother Ann had escaped Harvard's most brutal excesses on that occasion, but her life was no easy one as she visited other

towns. From Littleton and Woburn she journeyed through Massachusetts and Connecticut, passing through or stopping at Norton,
Rehoboth, Stonington, Preston, Windham, Stafford, Enfield and
Cheshire. She arrived at Ashfield November 1 for what turned out
to be a full winter's stay, extending to the end of April, 1783.

Ashfield appears to have been kinder to Mother Ann than
most localities. She is said to have attracted six hundred believers
in the town and surrounding vicinity. Although hostility erupted
from some quarters, Ashfield authorities protected the Shakers'
right to worship. Mother Ann returned to Harvard the first part of
May and remained for two months attending to the believers in
Harvard, Shirley, Woburn and other places. The fact that she was
unmolested for even a short time may reflect the sobered temper of
townspeople who had experienced the brutality of the previous
summer.

In June 1783, a minor incident reignited the belligerent passions of the mob. One Sarah Turner, married to a deaf and dumb
man named Jude Carter from nearby Leominster, decided to
become a Shaker, and she prevailed upon her husband to take up
the testimony, extracting a confession of sorts from him through
sign language. What is more, she tried to get him to cut his hair in
the shortcropped Shaker style and to sell his silver shoe buckles for
something more necessary. Jude didn't want to cut his hair
because he thought people would laugh at him, and resisted parting with his stylish buckles.

One day, husband and wife went to Boston to do some mar-
keting, and Sarah induced Jude to sell his buckles. Returning
home, they stopped at Nathan Kendal's house in Woburn. There,
Sarah persuaded Jude to have his hair cut; but Jude was not willing to have it cut as short as in the typical Shaker style, "and seeing
a man the cut of whose hair suited him, he consented to have it cut
like that man's, which was accordingly done."[34]

Jude seemed pleased with his new Shaker friends and spent a
convivial evening—that is, until bedtime, "when he strenuously
insisted on lying with his wife."[35] Sarah, of course, said that this
was out of the question in a family of believers.

The next morning the dejected deaf and dumb man left for

home ahead of his wife. Coming to Harvard, Jude complained in sign language and by sundry gestures—apparently to anyone who noticed him—that the Shakers had robbed him of his silver buckles, his hair, and his wife.

This was enough to reactivate the mob, which converged on Elijah Wilds's house in Shirley on a Sabbath evening, June 1, 1783. Mother Ann and the elders were engaged in worship with other believers when the mob, led by Phineas Farnworth, James Pollard, Elisha Fullman, and Asa Houghton, encircled the building, blocking all entrances. One of the sisters, Molly Randall, obtained grudging permission to leave so that she could return home to her nursing child. She took the opportunity to alert the Grand Juryman of the town to the Shakers' plight.

The Wilds homestead remained under siege all night. At daybreak, the mob demanded that Mother and the elders come outside, but the Shaker leadership consented instead to admit four of their leaders. Eunice Wilds was instructed to prepare breakfast and Elijah Wilds even distributed bread and cheese to the crowd outside. Mother Ann's strategy was "to feed our enemies."[36] Elder James attempted to talk to the crowd, but he was seized by the collar and arms and had to be saved from choking by a brother who rushed to his aid.

These events were interrupted by the arrival of the Grand Juryman, Thomas Buckmour, and James Parker, a Shirley peace officer. The two officials restored order, but the crowd failed to disperse. Mob leaders pressed their demand that Mother Ann and the elders be turned over to them; negotiations went on for several hours.

Finally, the mob agreed they would leave peaceably if William Lee and James Whittaker would accompany them back to Harvard. They promised not to mistreat the two elders. On these conditions the two agreed to go, and the mob set off; David Meacham, Calvin Harlow, and other brothers decided to accompany the elders.

Soon after entering Harvard, the mob reverted to its old character. The Shakers accompanying the elders were made to retreat to Shirley, except Meacham and Harlow, who insisted on staying.

Ultimately, the mob seized both James Whittaker and

William Lee and announced a scheme to whip them. Men tied Whittaker to a tree,[37] and Isaac Whitney began scourging him across the back with a stick cut from the brush nearby, lashing him so severely that James' back was "all in a gore of blood, and the flesh bruised to jelly."[38]

Turning their attention to William Lee, they seized him but allowed him to kneel while he was whipped. Whittaker—despite his condition—leaped on William's back to protect him. A neighbor woman, Bethiah Willard, seeing this, threw herself on Elder James' back. For her courage, she was severely beaten and received wounds which left her scarred for the rest of her life.

Calvin Harlow, who had been pinned to the ground to prevent his interfering in the whippings, cried out, "See how you have abused that woman; you have exposed yourselves to the law."[39] Sobered by this thought, or perhaps satisfied that they had accomplished their objective, members of the crowd dispersed.

As these events were happening, Mother Ann—seven miles away at Elijah Wilds's house—is reputed to have commented to Hannah Kendal, "The Elders are in great tribulation, for I hear Elder William's soul cry to heaven."[40]

When the bruised and battered elders returned to Shirley that evening, Mother Ann and the others were shocked and grieved.

"Did they abuse you, James?" asked Mother Ann.

"I will show you, Mother," said James, and kneeling before her, he exhibited his wounds.

The Shakers attended to James. Their sadness was lightened by the belief that they were suffering persecution for Christ's sake. James is quoted as repeating the words of Jesus, "Father, forgive them for they know not what they do."[41]

Thus ended an incident which began with Jude Carter, a deaf mute, and his zealous Shaker wife, Sarah. A marble shaft today marks the place where James Whittaker was so cruelly abused. The inscription on the stone records that at that spot a Shaker was whipped in 1783.

Mother Ann and her party left the following month to return to New York. Persecuted along the way, the travelers arrived at Niskayuna "about 11 o'clock at night, September 4, 1783,"[42] two years and nearly four months after having set out on their New England mission. Mother Ann had spent twelve months of that time at Harvard or Shirley.

The ministry of Mother Ann resumed, attracting believers from widely scattered communities where her teachings had taken root. But the physical strength of Mother Ann and other leaders had been sapped by the abuse they had undergone. Ann's brother, William, died within a year; Ann herself survived only two months longer.

William was only forty-four at his death. Physically powerful, a blacksmith, he gave up an early career of soldiering to follow his sister, disavowing a worldly life and leaving his wife and son. "I love my Mother," he once said, "although she is my sister; yet she has become my Mother, and the Lord God has made me to love her."[43]

Following the death of her brother, Mother Ann seemed to sense that her own time was short, and she began to prepare her people, repeatedly warning that she was about to leave them. She grew weak without any visible sign of disease.

"Brother William is gone," she declared, "and it will soon be said of me that I am gone, too."[44]

Mother Ann died on the "8th of September, 1784, between 12 and one o'clock in the morning." Shortly before her death, she reputedly stated, "I see Brother William, coming in a golden chariot to take me home."[45] John Hocknell testified that "when the breath left her body he saw in vision a golden chariot, drawn by four white horses which received and wafted her soul out of his sight."[46]

Mother Ann's obituary was published in *The Albany Gazette* the next day: "Departed this life," it said, "at Nisquenia, Sept. 7, Mrs. Lee, known by the appelation of the *Elect Lady* or *Mother of Zion*, and head of that people called Shakers. Her funeral is to be attended this day."[47]

Brother Abijah Worster of Harvard helped to make her coffin, and Brother Eleazer Rand, the future leader of the Harvard–Shirley ministry, helped to dig her grave.

4. The Gathering

DISHEARTENED BY MOTHER ANN'S DEATH, believers nonetheless continued to meet at the Square House in Harvard and at the Wilds house in Shirley. The residences were only a few miles apart, and travel between them was extensive.

Believers drew some consolation from visits by the Shaker elders, including Father James Whittaker, who succeeded Mother Ann. Father James acknowledged Harvard's special role in establishing the Shaker gospel. Visiting the believers at the Square House after Mother's death, he stated solemnly, "Surely God is in this place, pull off your shoes; for the place where ye stand is holy."[1]

Father James seemed to possess an alternately harsh and compassionate nature. Though one testimonial described him as "boundless in charity," James Shepherd and John Partington refused to serve under his leadership. Whittaker was criticized as the "champion of that phase of Shaker fanaticism which could find nothing good or beautiful in family life."[2] Writing to his parents, he once referred to them as "a stink in my nostrils"[3] because they persisted in living after the flesh. He boasted that he had never wronged any woman and claimed he felt no more lust than a child unborn.

Conflicting with this view of Whittaker as a zealot are descriptions of Father James's gentleness with children. His popularity was also commented upon by Shaker apostate and critic Thomas Brown, who reported, "they really loved Whittaker."[4]

At the graves of Mother Ann and William Lee, Father James spoke feelingly of having lost two great friends, but he determined to keep the spirit of Mother Ann alive. During the three years of his ministry he visited all the communities where believers resided, and even extended the gospel to Maine and New Hampshire.

A Sabbath service at Harvard illustrated his style of preaching. Kneeling with a large assemblage of believers, he said, "I am a poor worm of the dust, and a very little one too; I feel, many times, as though I could crumble into the dust before God."[5] At Shirley, Father James prophesied, "There will be a famine, not of bread, nor a thirst for water, but, of the word of God; and you will be glad to pick up every scrap, and every crumb that ever fell from our mouths. People will yet see the time when they will be willing to crawl on their hands and knees to the ends of the earth, to hear the word of the Lord."[6]

Whittaker remained aloof from temporal controversies. During Shays' Rebellion, when debt-burdened western Massachusetts farmers marched in defiance of Boston creditors, Father James cautioned, "They that give way to a party spirit, and are influenced by the divisions and contentions of the world, so as to feel for one political party more than for another, have no part with me. The spirit of party is the spirit of the world, and whoever indulges it, and unites with one evil spirit against another, is off from Christian ground."[7]

(Whittaker's nonpartisan stance may have rankled Shakers such as Aaron Jewett, who had served in the Revolutionary War, rising to the rank of captain, and was a delegate from Littleton to the Continental Congress of 1779.[8] At least fifteen other Harvard-Shirley Shakers had served in the war and were not dispassionate men by nature.)

Father James made a last visit to Harvard and Shirley in the

Sun Inn, Long Millgate, Manchester, England, with flower shop at left on corner of Todd Street, or Toad Lane, where Ann Lee was born.
(Drawing courtesy of R.J.K. Cahill)

Banns of Marriage *Abraham Standerin and Ann Lees were Published on Sunday Dec.ʳ 20ᵗʰ 27ᵗʰ and January 3ᵈ 1762 the Said abraham Standerin —* of *this* Parish *and Town of Manchester*

N°
7
——— Blacksmith ——— and *Ann Lees ———* of *this* Parish *and Town of Manchester Spinster ———————*_were Married in this *Church* by *Banns* _____this *fifth ———* Day of *January ———*_in the Year One Thousand Seven Hundred and *Sixty One ———* by me *Maurice Griffith*

This Marriage was solemnized between Us { *abraham ✗ Standerin. mark* / *ann ✗ Lees mark* }

In the Presence of _____ *James Shepherd*
Thos Hulme

Banns of marriage, Abraham Standerin and Ann Lees. Abraham's surname alternately appears as Stanley. Ann's surname is commonly shortened to Lee.
(Courtesy of the Andrews Collection)

The Square House, built by Shadrack Ireland in 1769, once had what one sourc
called a crown roof. Windows at the upper left indicate the bedroom where trad
tion holds Mother Ann Lee stayed. (Courtesy of the Library of Congress)

The Elijah Wilds house, in a later photograph (Courtesy of Elmer R. Pearson)

Stone monument marks the spot where Father James Whittaker was whipped. The custom developed to place a stone at the site, which this Shaker sister is doing. (Photographs by the author and Fruitlands Museums)

The grave of Mother Ann at Watervliet. The original headstone is in safekeeping. (Photograph by the author)

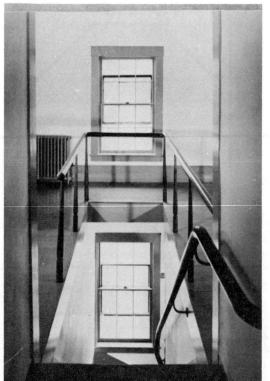

*Interior of the Shirley
Meeting House* (above) *with
antique lighting devices. The
wide span of the first floor
was supported by an upper
level suspension design typical
of master builder Moses
Johnson. (Photograph by Paul
J. Rocheleau, courtesy of
Hancock Shaker Village)*

*Interior staircase of the Har-
vard Meeting House, now a
residence. (Courtesy of the
Library of Congress)*

Earliest Shaker photograph, this disintegrating ambrotype of the Harvard South Family dates back to the mid-1800s. (Courtesy of Shakertown, South Union, Kentucky)

The Harvard Shaker Cemetery consists of ten rows of about thirty graves each with stone and "lollipop" monuments, the latter being iron markers. The iron markers, which were also used at New Lebanon and cost about two dollars, were adopted following a trip to Kentucky by Canterbury Elder Henry Blinn in 1873. (Photograph by Linda Wells)

Harvard Shaker Church Family, looking north, the only view in existence that shows the old office at right edge of photograph before it was moved to Fruitlands for use as the Shaker Museum. Other buildings at the right are the large new office building, the Meeting House, ministry, tailor shop, and Square House. Buildings at the left are the Second House and other buildings no longer standing. (Courtesy of Richard and Anne DeBoalt)

Plan of the Church Family, Harvard Shaker Village, drawn by Elder George Kendall, 1836. (Courtesy of the Index of American Design, National Gallery of Art, Washington, D.C.)

The Shirley Meeting House (Courtesy of Fruitlands Museums)

*Church Family building in Shirley still has bell in one of its cupolas.
(Photograph by the author)*

The South Family Barn, Harvard (Courtesy of Fruitlands Museums)

Harvard Shaker sawmill, built in 1808, continued in operation throughout the century. Products included lumber and railroad ties.
(Courtesy of Barbara MacKenna)

spring of 1787. He died on July 29, only thirty-six years old, the last of the English "witnesses" who had arrived in America aboard the *Mariah* and who had been called to serve in the ministry.

Father Joseph Meacham, then forty-six years old, took Whittaker's place as the new leader of the Shakers. Meacham's father had founded the Baptist Church in Enfield, Connecticut, inspired by the famous sermon of Jonathan Edwards, "Sinners in the Hands of An Angry God."[9] Meacham had served as a New Light Baptist minister in New Lebanon, where he had a wife and family. It was he who discovered the Shaker sect at Niskayuna, and he delivered a number of revivalist followers to the movement.

Mother Hannah Kendal quoted Mother Ann as having once predicted, "Joseph Meacham is my first born son in America. He will gather the Church in order, but I shall not live to see it."[10]

Meacham is indeed credited as the organizing genius of the Shakers, and is said to have patterned communal structure after the Jewish temple. One of his first acts was to elevate Lucy Wright to the lead in the female line, and this dual equalitarian leadership of the sexes served as a model at all levels of Shaker administration thereafter.

Communal societies were just then being organized, or established, first at New Lebanon and Niskayuna and then at Harvard and Shirley. Communities close to each other, such as Harvard and Shirley, were called bishoprics. Other bishoprics were established later at Canterbury and Enfield in New Hampshire; at Alfred and Sabbathday Lake in Maine; and at the three villages of Tyringham and Hancock in Massachusetts and Enfield in Connecticut.

All societies were subject to the central ministry at New Lebanon and each was governed by a dual hierarchy of male and female branch ministries. In addition, each family in each village was headed by two elders and two eldresses, who gave direction to an order of deacons and deaconesses and male and female trustees. The deacons were responsible for supervising agricultural and production activities and the trustees oversaw all financial dealings, including transactions with the outside world.

The ministry of each bishopric was required to visit New Lebanon at least once every year. This promoted Shaker orthodoxy and also encouraged considerable traveling among societies.

By the time Father Joseph turned his attention to establishing a bishopric in the communities of Harvard and Shirley, the Shakers there were beginning to be accepted by their neighbors. They were no longer included in Harvard's so-called Book of Warnings, as Eleazur Goodrich and other out-of-town Shakers were in 1783, in a roster of undesirables ordered to leave town because of apparent lack of income or employment. In Shirley, in May of 1785, the town had voted to abate the minister rates of the Shakers, renewing this vote annually until 1789 when they voted "to free them that are now called Shakers from paying a minister's rate for the future, whilst they are of that denomination."[11] Harvard town records note on March 5, 1787: "Voted that the society that meets at Aaron Jewett's Square House for public worship to have the money which they pay for schools."

In gathering the communities at Harvard and Shirley, a first step was to appoint a bishopric ministry. In 1791, Eleazer Rand and Hannah Kendal were named.

Eleazer had displayed exceptional courage on the missionary tour. It was he who threw himself on James Whittaker's back in Harvard, shielding Whittaker from the lash. He was only twenty-seven when he became elder, a destiny foretold by Mother Ann. Shaker history records that Mother Ann once confronted an angry mob congregated at Zaccheus Stephens's house and rebuked them for ridiculing Rand. Mother Ann called them a "wicked generation of adulterers" and warned, "take care what you say to a child of God! Touch not the anointed of God! He will have the keys of the Kingdom for the people in this place. He will be able to bind and to loose—he will be able to shut you out yet."[12]

Mother Hannah was thirty when she became eldress. Known as "the Valiant" in Shaker history, she had been a close traveling companion of Mother Ann. She shared in the persecutions of the missionary tour—both in Harvard and on the return trip to Niskayuna—and was a storehouse of anecdotal information on Mother Ann.

The nucleus of the community formed at Harvard comprised Isaac Willard, Zaccheus Stephens, and Abijah Worster. In 1777 they too had been absolved of the duty of paying their minister's rates by a vote of the townspeople—provided they produced "a certifiket according to the laws of this state that they belong to some other religious society."[13]

Willard not only gave the original eighty-six acres of land on which Ireland constructed the Square House, he also deeded over an additional one hundred acres to the Shakers in 1792; the land became the site of the South Family. In conveying the property to Shaker trustees, he alluded to "the love and good will I have and do bear to the church and society of Christians called Shakers . . . and their future well being, maintenance and upholding in Christian fellowship and communion as well as support."[14] At the same time that Willard provided the South Family acreage, Abel Jewett came forth with another substantial land donation, assigning fifty acres of his property.

Abijah Worster, though he could not make a significant material contribution, was a man of singular qualities. A Harvard native, Worster was reared as a Calvinist. He joined a church in the nearby town of Sterling when he was twenty-two, and transferred after a few years to the Harvard Church; he later became a Baptist, then joined with Ireland. He adopted Shakerism for the last half century of his life, and died at ninety-five.

During the Revolutionary War, Abijah was a fifer at the siege of Boston. He deserted, but this was probably not due to cowardice, for his physical courage was demonstrated in steadfast allegiance to Mother Ann: his loyalty cost him a whipping by the Harvard mob and occasional abuse elsewhere. Abijah seems to have been mortified as much by his struggle to control his gluttony as he was in subduing other fleshly appetites. He testified to a year-long struggle to control his hunger.

At the Shaker community at Niskayuna in 1784, he had a celebrated encounter with General Marquis de Lafayette, who was on a mission for General Washington to obtain the help of Indians in the Albany area. Lafayette attended a Shaker devotional meeting and observed the convulsing Abijah under a spell of "singular violent agitations." Moving to a seat beside Abijah, Lafayette watched him closely, to the point that Abijah became uncomfortable and felt compelled to leave the building. The persistent Lafayette followed. Abijah fled to the barn, but Lafayette kept on his heels. Finally, Abijah dashed off to a building where the elders were quartered, with Lafayette in close pursuit.[15]

Such anecdotes enhanced Abijah's image in the Shaker community. He became a legend in the society, and his longevity magnified his stature.

(Brother Abijah was one of a group of Harvard–Shirley Shakers who forfeited pension money for military service. Amos Buttrick of Shirley collected his pension funds for wounds and service before realizing that Shakers considered such awards blood money. When Buttrick decided in 1792 to give the money back to the government, a special resolve had to be passed by the Massachusetts legislature to allow him to do so.[16])

Elijah Wilds was the most prominent of the Shirley founders. Born in Groton in 1746, he moved to Shirley, prospered at farming, married when he was twenty-five and had four children. Two years before the Shakers came to town, Elijah began to be disenchanted with his religion. The Shirley Congregational Church appointed a committee on April 28, 1779, "to inquire into the delinquency in church attendance of Elijah Wilds and his wife, Eunice."[17] Elijah's family lived in a two-story frame house which he had built in 1771. It was to this house that Mother Ann came when she visited Shirley. (According to folklore, when the house was besieged by a mob, Mother Ann was at first hidden in a half closet in the southeast chamber and a bureau was pushed against the entrance.)

When the dual central ministry of Father Joseph and Mother Lucy at New Lebanon ordained that it was time for believers to gather in community, Elijah became the elder of the Church Family of Shirley and his brother, Ivory, headed the North Family. The property of Nathan Willard became the site of the South Family, and Willard became the society's first trustee.

In Harvard, believers gathered in four family groups. The Square House became the center of the Church Family; Isaac Willard's house was the location of the South Family, and other homes became the sites of the East and North Families.

The first priority in becoming a community was to gather all things together in one interest, both spiritual and temporal, having "all things common," as in the Bible. The Shakers first engaged in farming, for in the beginning there was insufficient food for their needs. It is likely that the Shirley Shakers had a more favorable agriculture situation at the start than did the Harvard community. The Shirley village sloped gradually from the river to a long ridge. Between river and ridge acres of fields were under cultivation. Agriculture was well established at the farms of Elijah and Ivory Wilds and John Warren and Nathan Willard, properties which were the nucleus of the village holdings.

In contrast, it was the remoteness of the northeast corner of Harvard that had appealed to Shadrack Ireland. It was quite distant from the center of town and approachable only by bridle roads. The area around the Square House lay in a hollow surrounded by hills crowned with woodlands, except at the north where it opened through a deep ravine. The uneven slopes were dotted with outcroppings of granite bedrock. The bottomland was largely swamp and grassland with a flat stream meandering south to north. Tree growth was chiefly red oak, together with some hickory, white oak, chestnut, pine and maple.

The Shakers immediately set to work clearing the land and straightening Bennett's Brook. Before long, the swampland was laced with irrigation channels.

Brethren improved the roads wherever necessary to provide routes of travel between family settlements and to improve access to surrounding towns and main highways. Travel was by foot, on horseback, or by wagon. Paths and roads led west from Harvard village through the Old Mill section to the Shirley village, passing over the Wilds bridge, a 116-foot-long narrow span over the Nashua River. This bridge, named for its builder, Elijah Wilds, was supported by stone abutments and two trestles. It carried considerable traffic between the two Shaker villages and was used by

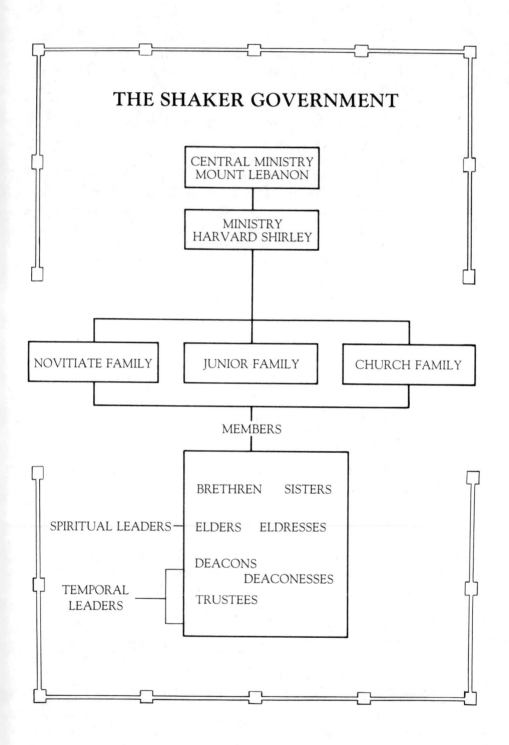

THE SHAKER GOVERNMENT

CENTRAL MINISTRY
MOUNT LEBANON

MINISTRY
HARVARD SHIRLEY

NOVITIATE FAMILY   JUNIOR FAMILY   CHURCH FAMILY

MEMBERS

BRETHREN   SISTERS

SPIRITUAL LEADERS — ELDERS   ELDRESSES

DEACONS
                DEACONESSES
TEMPORAL
LEADERS — TRUSTEES

the Shirley Shakers in bringing hay from their intervale lands east of the river.[18]

The donations of land from leaders like Elijah Wilds, though crucial, had to be matched by contributions from as many as possible for the communal experiment to succeed. In the Harvard Manifest journal covering the period 1791–1806, the names of 140 members are listed. Beside their names are ledger entries of the contributions of each: "three cows . . . 2 heifers with calf . . . 12 lbs. of beef and pork and a piece of cheese . . . a barrel of cider . . . box of applesauce . . . a bed . . . 6 earthen bowls, 2 mugs, teapot . . . a small pig . . . lb. of chocolate . . . 2 oxen . . . 2 swine . . . 13 lbs. of butter and the pail that it was in . . . 1 sucking pig . . . 2 baskets . . . 4 quarters of mutton . . . 10 bushels of corn . . ."[19]

Novitiate or probationary members often had to divest themselves of marital obligations. They had the option of either eventually becoming full members or withdrawing after experiencing the Shaker lifestyle. Junior Family members usually were new believers who were free of marital entanglements. They could contribute a portion or all of their wealth to the common interest, and the value of donated goods would be refundable if a member withdrew. Church Family members, on the other hand, signed a covenant pledging their wealth to the common interest and forfeiting future claims against the society. Donations of land, livestock, buildings, personal belongings, and money could be made.

The Shakers, after assembling possessions, immediately set to work building dormitories, shops, barns and meeting houses. The latter structures followed the design of gambrel-roofed meeting houses of master builder Moses Johnson of the Enfield, New Hampshire Shakers. He supervised the building of the Harvard meeting house as the community gathered in 1791, and that of the Shirley meeting house, which was constructed even before the society was formally gathered in 1793. The Shirley group grew to include, according to the census of 1790, sixteen men, nine boys under sixteen years, and thirty-eight women and girls—a total of sixty-three persons.[20]

Excerpts from the Harvard Manifest Journal convey the pace of activity in the first communal year:

February 19	Elizur Goodrich and Eleazer Rand came
April 13	Wednesday began to frame the meeting house
April 16	Eleazer Rand set out for Canaan [Central Ministry]
May 13	Eleazer Rand and Abijah Worster came from Canaan
May 16	Elder Joseph Meacham and Jethro Turner came
August 4	Joe Bishop, Daniel Tiffany and Able Shattuck came from Canaan and set out the night following for Canterbury. Same night Eleazer Rand Abijah Worster and Hannah Kendal come from Canaan
September 5	Job and two Daniels [Goodrich and Tiffany] set out for Sabbathday Pond
December 10	The meeting house finished and the ministers moved into the same
December 30	John Windley come from Canterbury and brot a clock for the meeting house.[21]

The Harvard meeting house was raised with reverent silence in early June and was first used for a meeting on January 22, 1792. Subsequent journal entries record the building of the first house, blacksmith shop, horse stable, women's shop, store, second house, barn, and other structures.

The frame of the Shirley meeting house was raised on October 31, 1792. Construction resumed the following spring, work was completed in the fall, and Father Eleazer conducted the first meeting there on October 27, 1793.

The Reverend William Bentley, pastor of the East Church in Salem, Massachusetts, visited both communities in July 1795, examined their new meeting houses and other buildings, and recorded his impressions in his diary. He first called at the Shirley village and mentions being shown the greatest hospitality by "Mr. Elijah Wild and his quondam Wife, now sister."

Bentley continued, "We first viewed the meeting house, which drew our attention, because beautifully painted white on the sides & even over the roof."[22] He said the building had green doors and deep blue woodwork, and chocolate-colored movable benches that could be placed around the room to clear the floor for a dancing area. There were two stoves inserted into chimneys at the ends of the buildings. He was not permitted to visit the apartments of the elders upstairs.

Bentley viewed the men's side of a dormitory, toured the village foundry and other shops, and examined the products of the women's looms. Bentley seemed to think the women more pleasant than he expected but was hardly enthusiastic about their appearance: "They were not extremely emaciated, but we observed none of full habits."[23]

Bentley was received by "Mr. Jewett & Mr. Willard" at Harvard and was entertained at the Square House with its "crown" roof. (Elder Eleazer was away when Bentley called, having left that morning to visit the Shakers in Maine.) He saw buildings being constructed and a network of gardens under cultivation. He estimated the Harvard community had one thousand acres and about two hundred members.

When Bentley visited in 1795, believers were fully organized. The covenant composed by Joseph Meacham that year was being copied in the communities and signed by members of the Church families. The covenant stipulated that members join freely and voluntarily, that any property or goods contributed be free of debt, and that each member receive an equal share and responsibility in the joint interest. Minors and children were not to become members or be accepted for care in the community unless consent was given by parents or guardians.

Father Joseph visited the Harvard bishopric for the last time in July 1796. Then the pages of the Harvard Journal record this entry: "August 16 Elder Joseph Meacham deceased." As the chief architect of Shaker communism, he had managed during his nine-year stewardship to gather all the communities of the Northeast into gospel order.

Among Father Joseph's other accomplishments was the first published statement of Shaker belief, entitled *A Concise Statement of the Principles of the Only True Church According to the Gospel of the Present Appearance of Christ.* The statement divided history into four epochs, called dispensations. In each of these dispensations, God's grace was given to man: first, in the promise of Abraham, second, to Moses, third, to Israel in the life of Christ, and finally, to modern man in the Second Appearance, or last display of grace to a lost world.

Believers concentrated on uniting themselves during the period of gathering and did little proselytizing among outsiders. As one history put it, "the testimony was withdrawn from the world about the year 1785, and was rarely opened to any until about the year 1798."[24]

5. Millennial Church

THE SHAKERS IN THE BISHOPRIC at Harvard and Shirley had gathered in communities which were firmly grounded in the Shaker creed. The doctrines most evident in their daily lives, of course, were communalism and celibacy; other tenets included belief in a dual deity, composed of a male and female element; a dual messiahship and the Second Coming of Christ; confession of sin; withdrawal from the world; pacifism; and equality of the sexes.

The Shakers claimed that celibacy was the cross one elected to bear in order to aspire to the state of spirituality forfeited by Adam and Eve, who partook of the forbidden fruit of sexual coition. This sin of disobedience, together with the indulgence of lust, corrupted humanity's ability to propagate, a faculty that initially was as innocent as eating and drinking. Adam and Eve revealed their shame by covering themselves with fig leaves. Ever since, the Shakers argued, despite matrimony and other attempts to sanctify it, sexual gratification has been accompanied by shame, by secretive means, and by retreat to darkness.

According to Shaker doctrine, humanity possessed sexual

faculties solely for purposes of reproduction. Because also endowed with superior wisdom, mankind should have been able to rise above the level of the animals, which mated according to the laws of times and seasons. Instead, man debased himself below the level of other creatures, gratifying his lusts at all times, even when the courses of nature forbade it.

Shakers criticized "the filthy custom" of husbands and wives constantly lodging together. Citing the ancients of the Old Testament, the Shakers noted that Scripture speaks of Abraham's tent and Sarah's tent—not of a single tent for cohabitation—and of Jacob's tent and Rachel and Leah's tent.

The New Testament also encouraged the Shakers in their view of celibacy. Jesus is quoted as saying that there were those who made themselves eunuchs for the Kingdom of Heaven's sake (Matt. 19:12). Saint Paul exhorted the unmarried to follow his example and remain unmarried—adding, however, "but if they cannot contain, let them marry: for it is better to marry than to burn" (1 Cor. 7:9).

The Shakers agreed that marriage was better than other outlets to lust. "We readily admit that the institution of marriage is useful in its place; because it has a tendency to prevent many evils in society which could not otherwise be avoided. And for mankind, in their present state, it is absolutely necessary. . . ."[1]

Mother Ann told those that were married, "You ought to love one another in the Lord." To the man she would say, "Be kind to your wife," and to the wife, "Be subject, and obey your husband in the Lord: it is according to the doctrine of the apostles."[2]

Though the Shakers tolerated marriage among the world's people, they contended that the aim of believers should be in regeneration of the spirit and not generation of the body. In answer to the assertion that God created male and female for the obvious purpose of procreation, they insisted that man was also blessed with a superior command which, if the laws of both God and nature had not been violated, would have allowed man to progress to an exalted state.

Objectors to celibacy contended that it should be enough that married couples did not abuse their privileges. But Shakers believed man could not simultaneously follow Adam in the work of physical generation and Christ in the work of spiritual generation. The fact that the ancient patriarchs and prophets were not celibate only meant that Jesus had yet to come and set a good example. Even the contemporaries of Jesus and the early Christians could only do their best according to the spiritual light then available—pending the Second Coming.

Their final rebuttal was to the argument that celibacy, if universally practiced, would result in the extermination of the human race. Those who advanced this argument were said to be more concerned about the threat to carnality than to the fate of mankind. Besides, the Shakers said, there could be less merciful ways for the world to come to an end. Finally, the concern was considered hypothetical, for universal celibacy was not at all probable. "The Great Architect has diverse grades of workman," it was explained. One Shaker apologist addressing the subject of celibacy in the nineteenth century even added that Malthusian threats of overpopulation and mass starvation supported celibacy.[3]

The communal life of the Shakers, based on the sharing of property and goods, also clearly displayed the Shaker work ethic. Work was necessary for community and thus deserved to be performed with efficiency. Shakers at work made every task a prayer. Mother Ann had instructed her followers, "Put your hands to work, and your hearts to God."[4] Mother Ann had experienced intimately the lot of the laboring class; reverence for efficiently performed work was ingrained in her. "Do all your work as though you had a thousand years to live, and as you would if you knew you must die tomorrow,"[5] she taught.

Anyone who was old enough and able-bodied worked. Men and women, children, and the aged worked. The ministry also did a daily stint in the shops or fields. Believers were encouraged to learn a variety of skills and to rotate tasks so that none became monotonous. Shakers worked at a steady but not exhausting pace; they ate well and got plenty of rest. Shakers, living and working as a group, benefited by one another's inventiveness and responded to the unique challenges of dormitory living and communal eating by devising new processes. Shaker ingenuity became proverbial.

The status of the female in the Shaker community was clearly superior to that of most women at that time. A female Shaker was not considered a male chattel and her position in the church was one of equality with men. Women owed their position to Mother Ann, of whom it was written: "In her was first wrought the complete redemption of the female and through her ministration a way was opened for the restoration of the female character to its proper lot and dignity, from which it had been degraded by the transgression of the first woman."[6]

Mother Ann's perceptions and her example served as models for the Shaker woman. Mother Ann was quoted on such topics as cleaning house, rearing children, and teaching table manners. Some of her sayings assumed the status of proverbs. Once she came into a room where a Shaker sister was scrubbing the woodwork. "Clean your room well," she said, "for good spirits will not live where there is dirt. There is no dust in heaven." At another time, she admonished, "Do not omit your washing till the latter end of the week; but do it on Monday, and set good example before the world."[7]

Mother Ann had strong feelings about wasting food. Once, she came to a table where several were eating. Taking a bone from the platter, she gave it to one seated nearby, saying, "Take this bone and pick it clean, and learn to be prudent."[8]

"I have a number of times seen Mother wait till the multitude had done eating, and then go to the table, with a mild and pleasant countenance, and there make her whole meal out of the fragments," a contemporary, John Farrington, testified, "I have seen her walk from end to end of the table, picking the bones after us, and eating the broken bits of bread which the multitude had left. Again, after the people had been eating spoon victuals, I have seen her gather the remaining driblets into one dish, and eat them with singular marks of thankfulness. This she often did, not only at home, in her own family, but also abroad, among the people where she visited; and she often took such opportunities to teach prudence and economy. Sometimes, the Elders, or some others, would urge her to have something better; but she would reply, 'It is good enough for me, for it is the blessing of God, and must not be lost. You must be prudent, and saving of every good thing which

God blesses you with, so that you may have wherewith to give to them that stand in need.' "[9]

Mother Ann's precepts instructed every department of Shaker life. She had warned her followers to refrain from intemperate drinking of cold water on warm days and to avoid having dogs in the house, since dogs were sources of evil spirits which children in the household might "catch."

She left a litany of advice on the rearing of children. "When children are put to bed," she stated, "they ought to be made to lie straight, to prevent them from growing crooked." She was insistent that children be kept clean and neat, but she showed impatience with one mother who had adorned her child in bows and ribbons. "You had better take those things off," she advised the mother, and "lay aside all superfluity, and dress in modest apparel. The more you indulge your children in such things, the more they will want, and if you bring them up in their pride, they will curse you to your face."[10]

She was negative on the subject of toys for children, saying that when she was a child her mind was taken up in the things of God, so that she saw heavenly visions instead of trifling toys. "Let them [children] look at their hands and fingers," she told parents, "and see the work of God in their creation."[11]

Some of her advice reflected her own prejudices, but much represented the standard wisdom of the ages: "You may always remember," she told her followers, "that the reproof of a friend is better than the kiss of an enemy."[12]

Celibacy and communalism were conditions not to be taken lightly, for husbands were separated from wives, parents from children. A lifelong commitment extended even to the grave; male and female cemetery rows preserved chaste eternal sleep. Elijah Wilds and Eunice Wilds were further segregated, for she was buried in Harvard and he in Shirley. So it would be for many former spouses.

Cemetery building came of age in the Shaker villages as the new century was about to begin. There had been deaths among believers from the very first. Burials and reinterments from earlier resting places are recorded as early as 1792 in both Harvard and Shirley, in the plots eventually consecrated as Shaker graveyards. An acre of land was provided for the Harvard community by Jeremiah Willard for $13.12. In order to erect a stone wall around the land, twenty-five of the Harvard brethren labored for eight days, assisted daily by four yoke of oxen. The task was completed in early November, 1799.

Shirley's cemetery was actually in Lancaster, in a field a few rods from the Shirley border. Rough slate markers from a quarry nearby, often inscribed only with initials, marked the celibate graves running in rows north and south.

Despite deaths, membership in the Shaker villages rose to about one hundred apiece as the nineteenth century began. Communities became prosperous. Pooling resources, property and skills, the brethren and sisters soon had large tracts of land under cultivation. There were neatly laid out streets lined with snug houses, ample barns, and inviting shops.

Carpenters, masons, blacksmiths, shoemakers, clockworkers, and cabinetmakers toiled diligently. Craftsmen skilled at making horsewhips, cartwheels, hammers—even surgeons' instruments— are recorded in the communities. There were makers of clay pipes (possibly the proteges of Shadrack Ireland, who was said to have been adept in the art of pipe making).

Most of all, the Shakers farmed. Shirley's several hundred acres were bountiful in crops of rye, corn and flax. Harvard's rugged fields yielded onions, parsnips, potatoes and cabbages.

Shaker women performed the usual domestic work. They did the housekeeping, cooking, sewing, knitting, washing and ironing. They also had their own shops. Chores were rotated monthly, and the journals constantly recorded that one sister "went into" the kitchen and another sister "went out."

Olive Wilds wrote in her diary that in one year she worked in the kitchen nine weeks, spun 370 skeins of yarn, carded 136 skeins by hand, doubled and twisted 152 skeins, knitted 13 pair socks, 19 pair of gloves, sewed eight days, ripped old clothes one day, picked wool four days, twisted yarn four days, pulled flax one day, washed yarn one day, washed every Monday of the year except five, ironed every week, scoured floors three days, and visited four days.[13]

Despite celibacy, women continued to be relied upon for the care of children, for nursing, and for teaching. The maternal instinct was not denied.

One notorious incident indicated that some of the workers gave of themselves grudgingly. On the night of March 3, 1802, a handful of dissatisfied Shirley brothers participated in a drunken takeover of the meeting house. The offenders included Peter Perham, Eleazer Robbins, William Blanchard and Aaron Lyons. (Perham had been mentioned in the account of the Reverend Mr. Bentley as the believer who greeted him in his Shirley visit in 1795. At that time Perham acted the role of overseer and village guide.) Perham and the others had contributed to the building of the meeting house; on that pretext, they occupied the structure and maintained an inebriated sanctuary there for four days, breaking furniture inside and barring the door to anyone attempting to enter. On the fifth day, on the complaint of trustee Nathan Willard, they were arrested. The liberation of the meeting house provided a local spectacle; about one hundred people assembled to witness the heroics of Constable William Going and a corps of officers. The barricaded interlopers, yelling taunts at authorities, refused to vacate. Finally, the dauntless Constable Going ascended a ladder, broke an upper-story window, and climbed inside.

According to Shaker accounts, "Robbins aimed at him [Going] a blow with a deadly weapon, which would have taken effect had not his murderous arm been withheld by his coadjutor, Perham, who knew the consequences of such resistance better than Robbins did."[14]

Robbins and Blanchard were taken into custody as Constable Going and his men invaded the building. Lyons was not immediately found; he had somehow fled. Perham retreated to the garret and hid in a closet, but he was rapidly seized. The miscreants were eventually brought before Justice Joshua Longley and remanded for trial at the next session of criminal court in Concord. They were never indicted by the Grand Jury, however, and

the Shakers intimated that Perham had bribed the district attorney. Perham tried to sue the Shakers for malicious prosecution,
but the defendant society was exonerated.

The incident was an unsavory one, hardly characteristic of
life in a Shaker village. In the words of the Shakers, it seemed that
the culprits were cursed with the "warring gift."

While the Shakers prospered in the worldly sense, the journals speak of a revival in 1807 which was marked by spirited
meetings in the bishopric. One pre-midnight meeting included
"singing, lively dance, sitting on the floor" and other "gifts." In
the meeting, which was conducted at the Square House, Father
Eleazer recalled that during the "first of the Gospel, great
numbers would collect at the house.

"Sometimes," said Father Eleazer, "many would be knelt
down around the house, praying for repentance and forgiveness of
their sins; and others under the trees opening their minds. And all
these precious gifts and power that we have received come from
our Blessed Mother, Blessed Father William, and Father James,"
he said.

Meetings seemed to follow a spontaneous format. Members
would collect for a "regular" meeting, but "before long they
would be set down on the floor; speaking in tongues, walking the
floor, leaping and turning . . . ," according to a Shaker journal.
Said Father Eleazer, "This shaking came to shake out that which
was wrong, that we might inherit the Kingdom of Heaven."[15]

Father Eleazer died in 1808, a few months following the
revival. Assisted by Mother Hannah, he had presided over the first
seventeen years of the bishopric. During that span, the Shakers
became an accepted—even welcome—presence in the region.

John Warner took Rand's place as senior elder, and affairs of
the village proceeded. The bishopric acquired land in the Monadnock Mountain region of New Hampshire, thanks to gifts from Elijah and Ivory Wilds. They also purchased land in Dublin, Jaffrey,
and Marlboro, New Hampshire. This land, and Shaker land inside
the Massachusetts border in the Bush Hill section of Ashburnham,
was used for pasture.

The wording of Elijah's deed typifies that of Shaker philanthropies: "For and in consideration of the Love and Goodwill and Regard I have and do bear unto the church and society of Protestant Christians called Shakers in the above said Town of Shirley and for their future well being maintainance and upholding in Christian Fellowship and communion as well as Support do give grant convey and confirm as a free gift and donation unto . . . said church . . . forever for the use and purposes hereafter mentioned and intended . . . for the express and only uses and purposes of Supporting the Gospel and for the help of the poor the widows and fatherless that may be real objects of charity and for the education of the Children of said Church and Society and for the help and Support of all others that may believe and Unite with them as the Gospel may Require and for other pious uses."[16]

Harvard land holdings were regularly augmented by gifts. In 1815, Seth Babbitt donated land to be occupied by the East Family. He had owned the adjoining farm and lived there with his wife and two daughters, one of whom, Tabitha, would become famed as an inventor. When the daughters persuaded their parents to join the Shakers, Seth swapped his farm for the East family land and deeded it to the society. His former property became the town poor farm. (Brother Seth became a Shaker trustee, but he lost his sanity in 1821, had to be placed under restraint, and was relieved of his position of responsibility. Four years later there was talk at town meeting of his treatment, accompanied by charges of cruelty or neglect. Shaker authorities were summoned in to court, but, before the matter could be resolved, Babbitt died.[17])

The bishopric was centered in Harvard and Shirley, but Shaker holdings expanded well beyond community borders. The Shirley Shakers had vast holdings extending to Ponakin Hill and Goatham sections in North Lancaster, and the Harvard Shakers spread a couple of miles into Groton in areas known as Sandy Pond and Snake Hill, where rattlers once roamed. In 1808, Harvard Shakers built a sawmill on Bennett's Brook near Littleton where the North Family was centered. The Shakers operated the mill for the remainder of the century, producing large quantities of lumber and, eventually, railroad ties.[18]

In 1816, Mother Hannah died[19] and her place was taken by

Eldress Rachel Keep, who was much beloved during her six-year tenure. Those in the ministry succession built upon the foundation Father Eleazer and Mother Hannah had established.

There was still much to invigorate the original commitment. The villagers were convinced that they walked upon ground hallowed by the earlier presence of Mother Ann. Early believers pointed to an iron ring, implanted in an enormous elm tree at Elijah Wilds's house, where Mother Ann tethered her horse. The believers in Harvard proudly preserved Mother Ann's rocking chair and showed the room in the Square House where she stayed. There were remembered places, here and there throughout the countryside, where the early persecutions had occurred.

Following the death of Father Joseph, the central ministry was dominated by Mother Lucy Wright. A native of Pittsfield, she had married a young merchant from neighboring Richmond, Elizur Goodrich, when she was eighteen, and had been led into Shakerism by her husband's conversion; she was with Mother Ann on the missionary tour.

Mother Lucy orchestrated the growth of Shakerism outside the Northeast. Early in Lucy's matriarchal rule, believers recalled the prophecy of Mother Ann—made repeatedly during her ministerial travels—that there would be a great work of God which would take place "at a great distance in the southwest,"[20] a work which she predicted that she would not live to witness. As it happened, in 1799 conditions arose favoring a new missionary endeavor in Kentucky and neighboring states. A series of religious manifestations—the frontier phase of the Second Awakening—excited the attention of religionists. The central ministry, alerted by newspaper accounts of the phenomenon, recognized it as the fulfillment of Mother Ann's prophecy. In 1805, Mother Lucy sent three of her most gifted lieutenants—Elder Benjamin Seth Youngs, Issachar Bates and John Meacham (Father Joseph Meacham's son)—to investigate. Their journey brought about the eventual founding of Shaker communities at Pleasant Hill and South Union in Kentucky and at other sites in Ohio and Indiana. Though some of these societies were short-lived, several flourished and came to rival in importance the Shaker communities of the Northeast.

The exploits of such persons as Bates, the leader of the trio of missionaries sent out by Mother Lucy, were followed with intense interest. Bates was known personally by the believers everywhere. It was said that Bates traveled some 38,000 miles, mostly on foot, through the wilderness of early America, planting the seed of Shakerism.[21]

At the same time, Mother Lucy maintained contact with older societies through regular pastoral visits. She instructed the believers in perfecting the form of worship, particularly structuring the ritual dances. Mother Lucy's frequent visits helped to shore up the faith of believers; her presence served as a link to the early founders now dead.

In addition, Mother Lucy was active as a defender of the Shaker faith. Apostates Valentine Rathbun and Amos Taylor had published denunciations of Shakerism. A book by Thomas Brown entitled *An Account of the People Called Shakers* appeared in 1812 and attempted to discredit the Shakers. In 1815, one Mary Marshall Dyer sued the Shakers, claiming the society had taken her husband and three children and her property from her. The Shakers responded by publishing testimonies from contemporaries of Mother Ann and the first elders, among them Elijah Wilds, Abijah Worster, John Warner, Hannah Kendal and Lucy Wright. In these testimonies, charges against the Shaker founders of lewdness, intoxication and witchcraft were dismissed as preposterous.[22]

Mother Lucy died in 1821, thirty-seven years after the death of Mother Ann, after a quarter century as head of the ministry. Lucy had brought Shakerism nearly to the summit of its powers, fulfilling a prediction made by Mother Ann that converting Lucy to Shakerism "would be equal to gaining a nation." Harvard Shaker Roxalana Grosvenor wrote years later, "At no time has the Church been more prosperous than during the twenty-five years of her administration."[23]

A few months after Mother Lucy's death, the so-called

Millennial Laws were circulated among the communities. A codification of bylaws formulated by Father Joseph and Mother Lucy, the Millennial Laws prescribed such diverse departments of village life as duties of trustees, consulting physicians, intercourse between the sexes (so worded), language, going abroad (which meant anywhere outside the village), burial rites, fire prevention, orders concerning beasts, and color schemes for buildings.

The Millennial Laws were never printed, but copies rendered in exquisite calligraphy were kept by the ministry in the Harvard bishopric.

Schools were set up in the Harvard bishopric as soon as the Shakers became settled—local precepts and bylaws notwithstanding. Some families entered the communities with as many as a dozen children. Not all families were accompanied by both parents, and some children were left at the community as orphans; the villages might be considered the first orphanages in America. Boys and girls were schooled separately, the girls in the summer and the boys in the winter.

The curriculum was specified in the Millennial Laws: "Spelling, reading, writing, linnear drawing, English grammar, composition, arithmetic, mensuration, the science of agriculture, agricultural chemistry, physiology, a portion of history and geography, music, moral science, good manners, and true religion, are sufficient as general school studies, for children among Believers."[24]

Higher learning was available upon the judgment of the ministry and the elders. According to the Millennial Laws: "No members but those appointed by the lead may study physics, pharmacy, anatomy, surgery, law, etc. and phrenology, mythology, mesmerism, and all such sciences as are foreign from Believer's duty may not be studied at all by Believers."[25]

Mother Lucy is credited with encouraging the system of schools. As superintendent, she appointed Seth Y. Wells, a teacher and an author of Shaker books. Wells himself addressed the children at Harvard in December, 1832. (An earlier distinguished speaker, Richard McNemar from Union Village, Ohio, an early leader of the Kentucky Revival and an influential force in converting much of movement to Shakerism, spoke in Harvard onAugust 29, 1829.)

The Harvard schoolhouse was next to the Square House; the school was designated District 8 by the town. Shirley's school, apparently limited to a classroom set up in one of the buildings, was Shirley's District 7; town reports indicate attendance averaged fewer than a dozen pupils.

The Shakers gave highest priority to moral training. A practical education was considered adequate for most children, and classical education desirable only if grounded in moral rectitude. "Learning without usefulness," they maintained, "is at best but mere lumber of the brain."[26]

Their pragmatism was rewarded. In 1828, Elder Joseph Hammond reported that the Harvard society could be considered in a "flourishing" condition. He bragged about a village complex that included a meeting house, a schoolhouse, ten workshops for males and females, seven barns, a tannery, a gristmill, and a sawmill, and other necessary outbuildings, all located within a distance of a mile and a half.[27]

The purchase in 1829 of the former Adams gristmill and dam on Nonacoicus Brook in the Old Mill area of Harvard, west of Shaker Village, marked the beginning on a large scale of the herb business in Harvard.[28] The millstones pulverized the herbs and spices. The herbs were used for teas, flavoring, and medicine. Herbs were first gathered in the wild by those who best knew the location of the most luxuriant growths of lobelia, pennyroyal, spearmint, peppermint, catnip, wintergreen, thoroughwort, sarsaparilla, dandelion, and other native plants. Sometimes a wagon load of children was deposited at a likely location to assist in the picking. Eventually certain herbs were cultivated in Shaker gardens.

Shakers manufactured rosewater from red roses, prepared and marketed garden seed, and made brooms, sieves and wooden boxes, spools, knives, chairs, palm leaf hats, turkey feather fans, and fancy goods. Harvard operated a bookbinding center.[29] Some members became proficient at caning chairs; others, at lettering gravestones.

Shirley's main income came from the making and sale of

applesauce. Other products included dish and floor mops, jellies, dry sweet corn, and maple sugar.

Harvard and Shirley villages had a combined membership of about three hundred and a total of about four thousand acres, plus random holdings in such places as southern New Hampshire. When Mother Lucy died, there were Shaker communities in eight of the twenty-four states. The future of Shakerism seemed bright indeed.

6. Mother's Work

SHAKER CONFIDENCE WAS BRIMMING as the sect entered the second quarter of the nineteenth century. The progress of the society seemed to be paralleling that of America itself, and optimists among believers could foresee Shakerism sweeping the nation.

The Shakers boasted a testimonial from no less a personage than Thomas Jefferson. Jefferson had been sent a copy of *Testimony of Christ's Second Appearing* and is quoted as commenting: "I have read it through three times, and I pronounce it the best Church History that was ever written, and if its exegesis of Christian principles is maintained and sustained by a practical life, it is destined eventually to overthrow all religions."[1]

By this time, the Shakers had the good will of most outsiders and were genuinely admired by many. Still, they learned to depend on their own resources, maintaining a system of mutual aid among communities. In November 1822, for instance, the Harvard and Shirley societies offered to furnish the glass for New Lebanon's second meeting house. In 1835, Enfield, New Hampshire gave Harvard thirty thousand white pine shingles for the South Family barn.

Certain individuals acquired widespread reputations for ingenuity. Such a one was Sarah Babbitt of Harvard, known as Sister Tabitha, who is credited with devising a circular saw. Sister Tabitha had noticed that half the motion of a reciprocating saw was wasted. While at work at her spinning wheel—for which she had already invented a new head—she got the idea of attaching saw teeth to the edge of a wheel.

Everywhere in the Shaker village there were examples of technological and domestic innovation. The Shakers saw no virtue in inefficiency and much merit in labor- and time-saving methods, provided they could be achieved without sacrificing quality. The result was a superior product that was valued in the marketplace. English socialist George Holyoake said, "They are the only dealers in America who have known how to make honesty pay."[2]

While the Shakers gained in public acceptance, they were loyal to their original religious principles. Those first believers still living reminded them of their heritage and made them feel proud. Job Bishop, for instance, while on a visit to Harvard and Shirley in 1827, recalled emotionally that he was the first to make known to the people at New Lebanon that Mother Ann had favored Father Joseph for society leadership. Abijah Worster, then in old age, was frequently called upon to recount the early days of Shakerism and the climactic happenings of the previous century.

The Shakers continued to attract attention by the uniqueness of their worship service. This did not always have flattering results; many of those who came were curiosity seekers, interested only in witnessing a spectacle. A traveler at a meeting in Shirley in 1831 reported his observations to the *Salem* (Massachusetts) *Gazette* in the issue of August 5. Arriving before the service, in the forenoon, he noted that "a large number of carriages of various kinds were ranged along the fence, most of them from the neighboring towns, but some from a considerable distance, and all freighted with curious visitors."

The traveler described the meeting house and the costumes of the brethren and sisters. Noting that the skirts of the sisters were not so long as to prevent the display of a "well turned ankle," he nevertheless was less than overwhelmed by the sisters' appearance.

"In point of beauty," he remarked, "it did not strike me that the world had suffered any great loss from their seclusion, for, not to be ungallant, a plainer set of girls and women could with difficulty be found."

On more than one occasion the audience was admonished by an elder not to jeer or laugh, the observer wrote. The dancing alone lasted more than half an hour. Afterwards, one exhausted young man cried out, "Oh! How happy I feel! I am convinced the Shakers are right and according to scripture. I am determined to act up to it. I am determined to subdue all my sinful lusts and carnal propensities, and persevere to the end. Yes, I will never give up!"

The elder lauded the young man's testimony, reported the traveler, and a number of the brothers and sisters chimed in with their approval. "I like that testimony"—"I'm glad that I'm a Shaker"—"This is happiness which the world can neither give nor take away"—were some of the exclamations.

Among the ranks of the Shakers was one Negro woman—undoubtedly Chloe Harris[3]—whose "shining morning face, round, vacant, good-humored, and black, contrasted curiously with the pure white of her own and the other dresses, and the sallow countenances by which she was surrounded," according to the news article. "Her devotional exercises were performed with an unction and fervor that showed her no lukewarm disciple of Terpsichore."

The practice of dancing as part of religious ceremony seemed incongruous to most spectators. Longfellow's wife compared a New Lebanon service to a "witch's sabbath."[4] The Shakers, however, cited various Biblical precedents. David had danced with might and vigor before the Ark of the Lord, and women had followed the prophetess Miriam in dance, to the accompaniment of timbrels.

As bizarre as the Salem traveler judged the Shirley meeting of 1831, it was comparatively tame in contrast to earlier years. A system of order had been introduced into the worship service, beginning in 1813 with the publication of a book of hymns, *Millennial Praises*, which substitued hymns in place of chants.

Mother Lucy had done her best to choreograph Shaker dances and had introduced motioning with the hands, movements designed to symbolize such actions as reaching out for divine gifts.

A popular dance march introduced in 1822 was called the Ring Dance. Four circles were formed with singers at the center. The circles represented the four dispensations of the Shaker faith: to Abraham, Moses, Jesus, and Mother Ann. Females danced in a clockwise motion; males, counterclockwise. Most of the dance patterns were vigorously executed to shake sin and temptation from the body.

Shaker worship always contained elements of the theatrical. These elements dramatically increased in the decade from 1837 to 1847, with intense spiritualism known variously as the New Era, Mother Ann's Second Appearing, or Mother's Work.

The first symptom of a mystical contagion in the Shaker world occurred at Niskayuna, New York, in August of 1837. Several young schoolgirls simultaneously went into a trance and began to shake with extraordinary intensity. This was repeated for several days; the same phenomena began to affect adults; the word spread, and there were similar manifestations in other communities.

At a meeting in early spring of 1838, Elder Philemon Stewart of New Lebanon became an "instrument" for direct communication from Jesus and Mother Ann. The Shakers were instructed to purge themselves of non-Shaker worldliness. Divinely inspired songs and other forms of creative gifts descended on the faithful, and believers were treated to visits by their Savior's parents, Almighty God and Holy Mother Wisdom, and by angels, prophets, and assorted historical figures, such as Alexander the Great, Napoleon, and George Washington.

However, much of the wisdom imparted was mundane. Shakers were advised to abandon such superfluities as silver pencils and were scolded for failing to repair damaged tools and for neglecting to clean muddy boots. Among the gifts received was a spiritual wine which believers quaffed, afterwards stumbling about in pantomimed drunkenness.

Amid this surfeit of spiritual blessing, the Harvard community suffered a distressing loss. Abijah Worster, the last survivor of

Mother Ann's original loyalists in Harvard, died, in his ninety-sixth year, on January 10, 1841. His funeral was attended with great ceremony, made even more resplendent as visualized by a spiritualist eyewitness. According to the Shakers ". . . an inspired Shaker girl stood at the door, to take down the names of those old friends from the spirit world, who were expected to attend the body to the grave, in honor of Father Abijah. This girl said there were all the first Shakers present. Father Abijah was very much gratified in seeing his old friends. The old man adjusted the head in the coffin, and asked Mother Ann if she thought he had changed much, she answered, no, Abijah, it looks well.

"We are told that Father Abijah marched out at the head of the coffin, singing a beautiful freedom song. The Pall Bearers were the Eternal Father, The Eternal Mother, Christ and Mother Ann. The brethren marched out of the house from one door, the sisters from another, preceded by the Elders, falling back a distance from the body to give room to the heavenly guests. The spirits lingered around the grave till their Brethren of earth had left the yard,—then Power and Wisdom, Christ and Mother struck up a lively dance, when all the spirits joined hands and danced merrily around the grave. At the close of the dance the Godhead crossed hands forming a seat for Father Abijah, and giving a glad shout spread their wings and ascended, followed by the heavenly host to Mother's mansion, where a banquet was in waiting to welcome the last of the first Fathers in Harvard to his final home."[5]

In spring 1842, the central ministry sent out word that the societies were to select a spot on some high elevation to be used for celebrating semiannual feasts in May and September. Each such location was to receive a special name. Harvard's place of outdoor worship was designated the Holy Hill of Zion; Shirley's, the Holy Hill of Peace. The communities were also given spiritual names; Harvard became "Lovely Vineyard" and Shirley, "Pleasant Garden."

Harvard's Holy Hill was approached by an avenue of rock maples, within easy walking distance of the village. The Shakers cleared the summit of the hill and levelled a half-acre plot by excavating the peak and using the fill to build up the slopes. The entire plot was enclosed, and a hexagonal area called the Fountain was outlined in the center, surrounded by a low fence. A marble slab, called the Fountain Stone, was erected at one end of the Fountain, inscribed in conformity to the instructions of the ministry.

On the back of the Fountain Stone were the words: "Written and placed here By the command of our Lord and Saviour Jesus Christ THE LORD'S STONE Erected upon this Holy Hill of Zion November 23d, 1843. Engraved at Harvard."[6]

On the side facing the Fountain was this message: "For the healing of the nations, who shall here seek my favor. And I will pronounce all people who shall come to this fountain, not to step within this enclosure, nor place their hands upon this stone while they are polluted with sin. I am God the Almighty in whose hands are judgment and mercy. And I will cause my judgments to fall upon the willful violator of my commands in my own time according to wisdom and truth, whether in this world, or Eternity. For I have created all souls, and unto me they are accountable. Fear ye the Lord."[7]

During the two years following the pronouncement from New Lebanon, Harvard journals are sprinkled with allusions to the preparations at Holy Hill.

"August 29, 1842 . . . Prepare and get ready to start for the Holy Hill of Zion. Start at half-past twelve P.M. The ministry, elders and biggest part of the brothers and sisters go; between eighty or ninety in all. We have a beautiful meeting here. Much speaking, singing, and dancing and marching. We get back to the first house at half-past six 'clock, having been gone six hours.

"November 14, 1842 . . . Cloudy and windy, wind N.E. The brethren of the Ministry and Elders, also the brethren of the Church, and families have a general turnout to work on the Holy Hill today—thirty-eight in all. The sisters of the Ministry, Elders, trustees and Family deacons, also Olive Hatch and Minerva Hill, bring our dinner out to us. The sisters waited upon the brethren while eating. After dinner we assembled round the fountain and sang an anthem called 'Gospel Baptism'—sung and danced some, and received the love and blessing of our Holy Savior. The sisters then returned to the house.

"February 5, 1843 . . . Note. The brethren of the Society worked on the Holy Hill 600 hours in the fall of 1842—so I have been informed this day by Brother John Cloutman who kept the account.

"June 24, 1843. The brethren that have been at work on the Holy Hill finished preparing the ground and sowed it down to oats and grass seeds.

"September 12, 1843. Elder Joseph Myrick has commenced lettering the marble stone that is to be placed at the head of the fountain on the Holy Hill of Zion.

"November 23, 1843. The Lord's Stone is erected on the Holy Hill. The stone was taken from the South House about ten of the clock and carried up on the Holy Hill and erected so as to stand correct at noon. The brethren of the Ministry and Elders' order assisted and eleven other brethren. Thomas Hammond and Elijah Myrick are putting up the fountain fence.

"May 5, 1844. We have our meeting upon the Holy Hill to-day."[8]

Meetings on Holy Hill were closed to the public. However, various descriptions were recorded by believers. The meetings included dancing, symbolic bathing in the holy waters of the Fountain, erection of an altar by the placement of bricks about the Fountain by believers, and elaborate "feasting" on spiritual food. The spirit world was liberally represented. At one meeting on Holy Hill, forty thousand spirits, including Indian chiefs, Biblical characters, and historical dignitaries were said to be on hand, encircling the hilltop in the manner of a Rubens painting.

An eyewitness account exists of a service at the Holy Hill in Shirley.[9] A procession of believers ascended on the north side in two platoons, with space between columns of brothers and sisters. Halting halfway at a bridge which spanned a small brook, an elder admonished all in words to this effect: Whosoever among us has anything against a brother or sister, let him or her not pass this brook until reconciliation is made.

There followed a round of explanations, apologies and hand-shakings. Then the believers "threw love" to each other, by throwing both hands toward one another and then drawing the hands back to the heart. The procession resumed in silence to the top of the hill. The summit was enclosed in a fence, with a gate. There were gravel walks about the Fountain area. An elder read the inscription. Believers prayed, gave testimonies, and marched around the monument, singing hymns. When the solemn ceremony was over, believers again formed in procession and descended the hill. Upon reaching their houses, they "threw love" to the aged and infirm who had stayed behind.

The new infusion of the spirit that began with school children permeated the rank and file membership. Ordinary believers became instruments of divine expression. But it remained for the ministry to interpret these manifestations, for they had been given spiritual spectacles in order to see more clearly. Thus was recorded Philemon Stewart's *Holy Sacred and Divine Roll and Book from the Lord God of Heaven, to the Inhabitants of Earth,* which was bound at the Harvard Shaker bindery and sent out "to the nations" on December 14, 1843. Another significant publication relating to the period, authored by Paulina Bates and called *The Divine Book of Holy Wisdom,* was issued in 1849 as the period of manifestations—Mother's Work—was subsiding.[10]

In addition to inspired books, visits from the hereafter, and a rash of newly composed hymns, Shakers received gifts of "spirit drawings." These were pictures that members were moved to create. The finer examples became masterpieces of American religious and folk art and depict symbolic fruit, flowers, chains, belts, doves, altars, crosses, angels, and other objects.

The years 1840 to 1845 brought unorthodox neighbors to the Shakers of Harvard and Shirley. At Fruitlands in Harvard, Bronson Alcott and his companion Transcendentalists conducted a utopian experiment; in Groton, an assembly of Adventist Millerites gathered to await the end of the world. Contacts among Shakers, Millerites, and Transcendentalists were numerous.

The saga of Fruitlands involved an attempt to find in simple communal living a "New Eden," which would unite man to God by relying on natural instinct and on intuition transcending sensory perceptions. The philosopher Alcott, a friend of Emerson and Thoreau, joined with a small group of other seekers, including

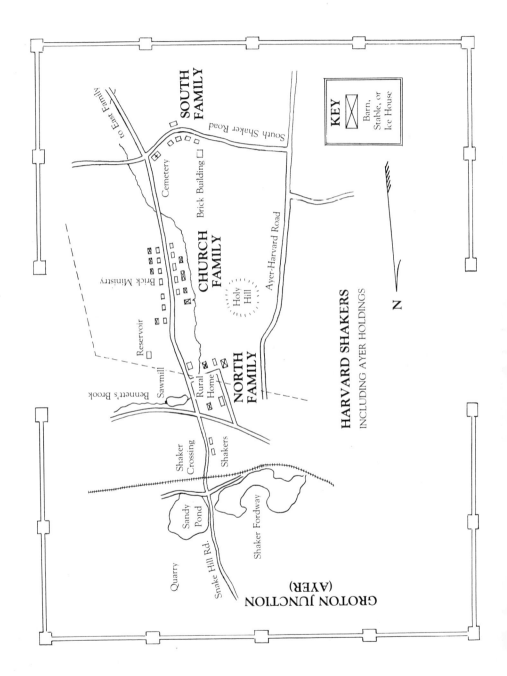

HARVARD SHAKERS
INCLUDING AYER HOLDINGS

KEY

Barn,
Stable, or
Ice House

N

SOUTH FAMILY

to East Family

South Shaker Road

Cemetery

Brick Building

CHURCH FAMILY

Brick Ministry

Holy Hill

Ayer-Harvard Road

Reservoir

Sawmill

Bennett's Brook

Rural Home

NORTH FAMILY

Shaker Crossing

Shakers

Sandy Pond

Shaker Fordway

Quarry

Snake Hill Rd.

GROTON JUNCTION (AYER)

79

the Englishman Charles Lane, and repaired to a secluded hillside farm in northwestern Harvard on June 1, 1843. Alcott, who was accompanied by his family, was forty-three years old at the time; his wife, forty-two. The Alcott children consisted of Anna, twelve; Louisa May, ten; Elizabeth, eight, and May, two.

The family attachments of the two leaders, Alcott and Lane, were a potential source of conflict as the highminded experiment proceeded and Lane began to press the issue of celibacy. Lane, who was estranged from his wife in England, was the father of a ten-year-old son, William, who was also part of the community. Others who became associated with the group included Joseph Palmer of Leominster, a man who had won notoriety after spending a year in jail for refusing to shave off his beard; Samuel Bower, a nudist who eventually found asylum in the Florida sun; and Isaac Hecker, who lingered briefly at Fruitlands before moving on to found the Roman Catholic Order of Paulist Fathers.

The back-to-nature movement at Fruitlands took peculiar forms. Members were not to exploit animals. This meant they were to abstain from the use of animal products, including eggs, fish, milk, butter, oil, and leather. They also rejected wool because it robbed the sheep of its property. They believed cold showers were healthy, even in winter. Their diet was to consist of fruit, grain, and water. The community banned the use of alcohol and even coffee, tea, and cocoa. Manure was not to be used in cultivation, because it fouled the earth.

Trying to make a livelihood with these restrictions proved quite a challenge. While the philosophers philosophized, it remained for the two most practical members of the community—Mrs. Alcott and the bearded Palmer—to make the most of their considerable domestic and agricultural resourcefulness. During the summer months, when Alcott and Lane should have been tilling the soil, they were too frequently occupied roaming the countryside in search of recruits and observing the activities of their fellow man. Among the places they visited were Shaker villages across town.

The visits of Transcendentalists to the Shakers are recorded in the diaries and letters of the Alcotts and in the journals of the Shakers. Anna Alcott mentions, for instance, that her father and

Lane went early one Saturday to the Harvard village, stayed all day, and brought home sweet things which they had purchased.

Lane and Alcott were favorably impressed by the Shakers, describing them in a passage of a letter written in August of 1843:

"On this topic of Family Association, it will not involve an entire agreement with the Shakers to say they are at least entitled to a deeper consideration than they yet appear to have secured. There are many important acts in their career worthy of observation. It is perhaps most striking that the only really successful extensive Community of interest, spiritual and secular, in modern times was established by A Woman. Again, we witness in this people the bringing together of the two sexes in a new relation, or rather with a new idea of the old relation. This had led to results more harmonic than anyone seriously believes attainable for the human race, either in isolation or association, so long as divided, conflicting family arrangements are permitted."[11]

Contrasting with this male viewpoint was the reaction of Mrs. Alcott, who wrote in her diary on July 2, 1843: "Visited the Shakers. I gain but little from their domestic or internal arrangements. There is servitude somewhere I have no doubt. There is a fat sleek comfortable look about the men, and among the women there is a stiff awkward reserve that belongs to neither sublime resignation nor divine hope."[12]

Lane wrote about the Harvard Shakers in an article printed in the Transcendental organ *The Dial*. Entitling his piece "A Day With the Shakers," he gave a sympathetic airing of the Shakers' views, quoting liberally from the book *Summary View of the Millennial Church*. He was, however, critical that the village engaged in trade amounting to $10,000 annually, which he felt was too great an involvement in money matters and reflected a lack of true simplicity.

"Their estate," he wrote, "does not at present produce a full supply of bread-corn; most of the members, except the children, consume flesh-meat; much milk is used; and the aged amongst them still drink tea, or coffee, and the like. For these reasons, some of their produce has to be exchanged, which occasions considerable traffic. To provide for their wants they also are extensive manufacturers of various clothing and other fabrics, and have to buy raw material to work upon, as well as to sell the goods when finished. These proceedings require more extensive interchange of money, and more frequent intercourse with the world, than seems compatible with serene life."[13]

In their frequent visits, Alcott and Lane conversed primarily with the leaders, notably with Elders Joseph Hammond and Joseph Myrick. The two philosophers were also said to have thought very highly of Olive Chandler, who at twenty-nine was gifted with charm and a fine mentality. Alcott indulged in long discussions with her on the mystical side of life; they felt that her insight was as keen as that of anybody at Fruitlands.

While philosophy bloomed in Harvard during the summer of 1843, the crops at Fruitlands withered. The harvest was modest, prompting the less committed among the Fruitlanders to conclude that the winter larder would be too spiritually seasoned. The same brisk autumn winds that whipped the leaves off the trees carried off the timid, and only the Lanes and the Alcotts remained. The time came to redefine the philosophical generalities that had glistened so indistinctly in the benign summer sun. Alcott and Lane clashed on the value of the individual family as an institution. Lane held that the family unit had a divisive effect on society, standing as an obstacle to communal betterment. Alcott, who subscribed to some of Lane's views in theory, became less resolute when the implications for his own situation had to be faced.

A discouraged Lane, summarizing the turn of events in a letter to friends in England, wrote that followers were deserting Fruitlands, that Mrs. Alcott had no inclination towards a larger family than her own natural one, and that he faced added indebtedness in behalf of the community. "You will perceive that I have . . . a small peck of troubles; not quite heavy enough to drive me to a juncture with our friends, the Shakers, but sufficiently so to put the thought into one's head. . . ."[14]

Finally, Mrs. Alcott, acting with unphilosophical decisiveness, announced that she would take her four girls to live in a nearby farmhouse rented for the Alcotts by a relative. Bronson Alcott accompanied his family; later in the winter they moved to a house in the center of Still River.

On January 3, 1844, a Harvard Shaker journal records this entry: "Charles Lain came here & brought his son William to live with us. Elder Jos. came with them and they all staid to dinner & supper." The father took up residence with the South Family and the son with the Church Family. There are a number of entries to show that the father frequently visited his son, and, just as frequently, made trips to Boston and elsewhere.

Lane went back to England after several months, leaving his son with the Shakers. Fruitlands was temporarily left in the care of the Shakers. It was later acquired by Joseph Palmer, who maintained his home there for the next twenty years.

Lane's association with the Shakers was short-lived. For some disputed reason, he had difficulty reclaiming his son. His problem resembled a situation involving the father of two girls left with the Shirley Shakers. The father, who was illiterate, complained that his daughters, the oldest fifteen, were held captive from him after he had entrusted them to their care. The father said he had signed a bond which he was told merely excused the Shakers from paying wages if the girls should leave the community.[15] Lane also argued that he had "articled" his son to the Shakers on their assurance that the document was only to prevent a claim for wages; Lane said he accepted what was told him and only learned afterwards that local reality did not match the moral premises he had endorsed. He said lamely that it was better to be sometimes cheated than always suspicious,[16] but in letters written to Emerson over a period of two years prior to William's release in 1848, Lane expressed his anger and frustration with the Shakers.

Emerson and the Alcotts were instrumental in extricating young William from the Shakers. The Alcotts gave the boy a home for a few weeks before his passage back to England was arranged. Thus ended the relationship between Fruitlands and the Shakers. The Alcotts had found their way back to Concord; Lane remained in England, married again, and had five more children.

Though Fruitlands was economically flawed, it is remembered with affection. In terms of numbers involved, however, it was insignificant on the social landscape as measured against the Millerite delusion, which also reached its climax in the rarefied atmosphere of 1843 and 1844. Followers of William Miller, a Baptist farmer-evangelist from Vermont, the Millerites prophesied the near approach of the end of the world. One of the Millerite encampments was in the town of Groton, at a site later occupied by the prestigious Groton School. A convention of Miller's followers and so-called Come-Outers was held there in 1840, a convention which Alcott and some of his Concord associates attended.

Miller spent his adult lifetime in the study of the Bible and based his prophecy on various passages in the Book of Daniel. He concluded that the world would end about 1843, sometime between the vernal equinoxes of 1843 and 1844. So persuasive was his message that he attracted an estimated fifty to one hundred thousand followers. Nearly half a million spectators attended the more than 120 camp meetings held throughout the country in the climactic summers preceding the promised Second Advent. Many people became so convinced of the imminent end that they sold or gave away all their possessions. According to persistent accounts—often disputed—numbers of people prepared white ascension robes and repaired to rooftops, hills, or treetops to await being "taken up." When the year passed uneventfully, a revised calculation set the final day as October 22, 1844. When that day also came and went, general disillusionment set in. Numbers of these Millerites joined the Shaker societies of Harvard and Shirley.

Anyone reading the history of this time would perceive that it had a unique quality about it, and especially was this true among the peoples of Harvard and Shirley. There was prophetic expectation, philosophical idealism, and Shaker spiritualism. The atmosphere was electric. But while Alcott's New Eden foundered and Miller's Second Advent sputtered, Mother's Work thrived. The disenchanted could find refuge in the Shaker villages, where a comfortable livelihood could be enjoyed in conjunction with lofty thoughts.

The Shaker star was at its zenith and would appear to remain so for another quarter century. But things were happening in the world even then that would arrest the progress of the sect and lead to its eventual decline. The introduction of the telegraph by Samuel F. B. Morse was ushering in a new era of communication;

President Tyler was opening the Orient to American traders; the railroad was linking rural and urban America; abolitionist sentiment was setting the stage for approaching civil strife; and gold lay ready to be discovered at Sutter's Creek, bringing on the rush to populate the West.

The Shakers would not disapprove of these developments. On the contrary, they exulted in the social progress of America and applauded technological advance. The Shakers believed in progressive revelation in matters spiritual and could not see why temporal enlightenment should not also be welcome. Their own economic structure, in fact, served as a crucible for inventive creativity.

Shaker journals record that on June 17, 1844, "We hear that the cars run from Boston to Concord to-day on the Boston & Fitchburg Railroad for the first time since it was finished as far as there."[17] Later that year—on December 10—there is an entry to the effect that Alvah Crocker, a Fitchburg industrialist instrumental in promoting the railroad, "informs us that the Company intend to give all the Believers in Harvard a free pass over the road when it is finished to Fitchburg."[18] Again, on December 30, 1844, a Shaker scribe reports, "The passenger cars run up to Shirley Village to-day for the first time. A screaming from the engine whistle could be heard almost every hour from seven in the morning till seven at night."[19]

While distant train whistles signaled a new tempo in the character of American life and commerce, forces were being exerted worldwide that would revolutionize society in other ways. At a conference in Germany in February of 1845, Friedrich Engels argued that a communist system could be profitable and practical. He cited the Shakers as a prime example in America of how such a community could be successful, neglecting to give attention to the religious orientation that was the foundation of Shaker communism.

The Shakers, meanwhile, went placidly on, interested in the world about them but disdainful of involvements that might sway them from their central spiritual mission. They looked confidently to the future, yet remained steadfast to their past. On November

10, 1844, we find this entry in the Shaker journals: "In the P.M. we march out to the spot where Father James was tied and whipped. The South Family join us when we arrive there and partake in the dutiful and commendable act of commemorating the sufferings endured by our Gospel ancestry."[20]

The Shirley Fountain Stone bears an ominous legend on its face (top). Photographed after the Holy Ground had fallen into disuse, it reads on its obverse side: "Written and placed here by the command of our Lord and Savior Jesus Christ. Engraved at Harvard. Erected July 15, 1844." The stone has long since disappeared.

(Courtesy of Erhart Muller)

(Courtesy of Lucy Longley)

Engraving of the Harvard Holy Hill of Zion, from David Lamson's Two Years Experience Among the Shakers, *published in 1848.*

Shaker spirit drawing "Wings of Holy Mother Wisdom, Wings of the Heavenly Father" with symbolic birds, trumpets, flowers, clocks, etc. and with trees and messages from Mother Ann Lee, Father William Lee, Father James Whittaker, Father Joseph Meacham, and Mother Lucy Wright.
(Courtesy of Fruitlands Museums)

The Shirley Church Family, as viewed from the south. Bellhouse at left is flanked by two buildings which still exist but have been moved to other locations. Buildings at right include the Meeting House (now at Hancock), the ministry, and the office building.

The Shirley North Family is dominated by the barn at the right and by the brick office building at the left. Shakers and possibly hired men labor in the fields in the foreground. (Courtesy of the Shaker Museum, Old Chatham)

The Old Mill Place, formerly the William Adams gristmill and dam on Nonacoicus Brook in Harvard, was purchased by the Shakers from Arna Wetherbee and was used by the Shakers for pulverizing herbs and spices. The Shakers sold the mill to Henry Hapgood in 1838. The mill was used for various reasons. This photograph was taken in 1870. The mill was destroyed by fire in 1888. (Courtesy of Fruitlands Museums)

Shaker or Phoenix Mill, as painted by an itinerant artist. The mill is at left, rooming houses are at center, and pedestrians can be seen on the roadway and bridge passing by Phoenix pond at the right. (Courtesy of the Hazen Library, Shirley)

Shaker Village street scene in Harvard, viewed from the north, with four yoke of oxen dragging a wagonload. (Courtesy of Louise Fletcher and Hancock Museum)

The last Shaker building in the North Family is this building at left, used as the office. The ell and the building at right are gone. The Harvard North Family office building straddled the town line of Groton, the southern part of which later became Ayer. (Courtesy of Barbara MacKenna)

THE RURAL HOME.

Allow me to respectfully call your attention to the advantages offered by the Rural Home as a refuge from the annoyances of city life and the summer heats. The Rural home is a substantial Brick Building, 90 x 50 ft., three and a half stories high. It was built for a dwelling for a branch of the family of Harvard Shakers, and the continuous and increasing applications from the cities for summer board, induced them to fit it up for that purpose. Its location and surroundings fill all the requirements for

A PERFECT COUNTRY HOME.

It is thirty miles from Boston, by Fitchburg Railroad, and one mile from the Ayer station, on the summit of a gentle rise, with shaded avenues and walks and pleasant drives in every direction, and whatever a farm contributes to make up the pleasure, in contrast with the dust and heat of the city. A more quiet and retired Home cannot be found in the state.

All those desiring perfect freedom from the exacting demands of fashionable customs of dress and society, can here be sure of finding their wants gratified. The appointments of the house are excellent; the halls are wide, the rooms large and airy, twice the size of ordinary hotel rooms, with dressing-rooms attached. A spring supplies the house with pure soft water. The table is supplied with the choicest production of the Shaker Community.

Those who wish to bring their teams will find the best of accommodations and care. There are sixteen trains each way daily, all stopping at Ayer Junction. Special rates for business men can be had by applying to the proprietor, and package and family tickets, with liberal discount, can be obtained at the Boston office, and also at the Home. Carriage to convey passengers to and from the Home on the arrival of the trains.

Those contemplating the quiet and comfort of this "Home" will do well to apply soon to secure their rooms. We invite you to a personal inspection.

Address JOHN H. SPRAGUE, Rural Home, AYER, MASS.

The Rural Home (above), *with the 1853 datestone plainly visible on the facade. This is undoubtedly a more accurate view of what the building looked like than a lithograph (opposite) which advertised the property as a health retreat and featured a much fancier porch. (Courtesy of the Society for the Preservation of New England Antiquities)*

Augustus Grosvenor (right).
(Courtesy of Barbara MacKenna)

Elijah Myrick as a young man
(Courtesy of Fruitlands
Museums)

Elder Simon T. Atherton
(Courtesy of Fruitlands
Museums)

7. Prosperity and Personality

M ID-CENTURY WITNESSED the greatest total membership of the Shaker society—about six thousand. This small fraction of the country's 1850 population of twenty-three million exerted, however, a disproportionate influence on the country. Distinguished visitors from throughout America and Europe visited them and wrote detailed accounts of their life and belief.

Scores of non-Shakers were exposed to Shaker thought. Besides those who became enrolled members, there were countless novitiates who stayed only briefly, including "winter Shakers"— those who "joined" the Shakers to escape the elements and left at the first sign of spring.

The Shakers never turned anybody away: "We have many calling to our doors to get bread to eat," a Shirley diarist wrote in January of 1858. "And many to get a home with us; perhaps some will finally be good Shakers. It is said to be very hard times."[1]

A Shaker diarist in Harvard gave a statistical view of that community's fluctuating membership, circa 1853: "In sixty-two years 422 became Shakers at Harvard. Decrease in sixty-two years—124. Returned to the world in sixty-two years—191."[2]

Celibacy certainly inhibited a stampede to join the Shakers. But there was security to be derived from Shaker membership. Clearly, the Shakers were prosperous. In Harvard, the herb business alone kept the community busy. At first herbs supplied only the community's own needs for medicine and food flavoring; now products were shipped around the country to such well-known firms as S.S. Pierce and Park and Tilford. By 1849, a foundation was laid for an herb house at the Church Family. The journal of Elisha Myrick describes the volume of activity during the first year that the herb house was utilized.

"The business this year is carried on by Elisha Myrick, aged 25, and George B. Whitney, aged 22, with the assistance of Isaac Myrick to gather herbs out from home and two sisters to pick over the herbs, viz., Mary Robbins and Charlotte Priest. We do our pressing and keep our stock of pressed herbs at the ministry's barn and pick our herbs and do other work at the yellow house. We distilled 165 gallons of peach water and made 134 pounds of ointment, 49 gallons of buckthorn syrup and pressed (between February 14, 1849, and February 14, 1850) 10,152 pounds of herbs, roots, etc. The sale for 1849 including all the herbs, and delivered to agents, amounts to $4,042.31 net.

"We raise, gather and prepare this year 5788 pounds of herbs, barks, roots, etc., which is five hundred pounds more than was ever culled before.

"The foregoing statistics," Elisha concluded proudly, "would be a good introduction, I thought, for the first journal I ever kept after having worked in the herb department 14½ successive years."[3]

Brother Elisha displayed typical Shaker enthusiasm for technological innovation. Commenting on his new herb-pressing machinery, he wrote, "Every improvement relieving human toil or facilitating labor [affords] time and opportunity for moral, mechanical, scientific and intellectual improvement and the cultivation of the finer and higher qualities of the human mind."[4]

The Myricks were a large family; Elisha's parents had come among the Shakers with no fewer than twelve children. His brother, Elijah, later distinguished himself. Although Elisha remained active in the herb department for some time, he eventually left the Shakers.

Another thriving Shaker enterprise was their seed business. Shakers were the first to market seeds in small packets. Shaker seeds gained a reputation for quality and high yield, and sales expanded rapidly; it was necessary to publish instructional leaflets.[5]

Also lucrative was the sale of Shaker medicinal herbs, which Shaker trustees sold to pharmaceutical pioneers McKesson and Robbins and to William Scheifelin and Company. Shaker herbs and patent medicines were a part of the nation's dispensary until this century, even after the 1906 Food and Drug Act restricted such products.

One of the more popular Shaker products was rosewater, which was used for flavoring pastry and for perfume. Red roses were an ingredient in the manufacture of rose cream, which was advertised as being effective in removing tans, freckles, pimples, moth patches, and sunburn.

At the Harvard herb house, there was a room where rosewater was distilled and stored in large demijohns. The community had a large field of enormous cabbage roses which were a gorgeous red when in bloom and apparently odorless, but, when weather grew warm, were almost overwhelmingly fragrant. They were gathered while the dew stood on them and then covered with salt, steeped for a day, and distilled, making rosewater.[6]

Shaker distilleries were not limited to making rosewater. Shakers at Shirley made elderberry wine before fermented drinks came to be frowned upon. The Shirley distillery was once raided by authorities, as reported on December 20, 1879, in the local newspaper *Turner's Public Spirit*:

"The quiet and inoffensive people of our Shirley Shaker settlement, and the people of the town, have been startled at the seizure of a still at the Shakers. It seems that from time immemorial the Shakers as well as many honest farmers in and around town, have on their premises an apparatus for distilling herbs, roots and fruits etc., which has been in use more or less, at intervals, all these years in an open and public manner.

"On Tuesday last the Shakers were very ceremoniously visited

by revenue officers Eldredge and Norcross of Lowell with Sheriff
Peter Arbell of Ayer and Officers Scott and Parker of Shirley, who
took away a still with a quantity of cider brandy to a place of
safety, to be disposed of, according to law. It has created quite a
sensation in this locality.

"Of course there can be no defense set up to defeat the government, but a plea of mercy with a statement of the circumstances
supported by a certificate from the influential and reliable citizens
to work out the cause of justice only. This case seems to have had
origin through some degenerate renegade rather than a refor-
matory act, or to further the cause of temperance."

Shaker patent medicines, like most such products, owed some
of their therapeutic powers to their alcoholic content. Cider was
an important beverage because it didn't spoil; it was as much a
staple as milk and water, which were often unsanitary.

Believers heeded the temperance movement in banning both
alcohol and smoking. They sympathized with the dietary views of
Sylvester Graham, father of the graham cracker and an advocate
of a diet of vegetables, fruit, and whole wheat bread. The Shakers
deplored the process of milling wheat which, they pointed out,
removed the live germ of the grain while making it lighter in
weight and color; what for countless ages had been the staff of life
became but a weak crutch.

Shakers recited the praises of oatmeal porridge and brown
bread but became disenchanted for a while with pie and
doughnuts and briefly swore off meat. Though pigs were still
raised to dispose of garbage, pork was avoided for a long time, and
Shakers claimed reduced incidence of cancer after renouncing
pork.

The Millennial Laws were difficult to obey completely. We
read that many of the older sisters, for instance, struggled to give
up their pipes; others had to contend with a sweet tooth. Though
transgressions of this sort were frowned upon, they were not cause
for expulsion. Pies eventually returned to the diet, and Shakers
devised revolving ovens so that pies would cook evenly.

The Shakers impressed their countrymen with innovations
and gadgetry. In addition to Tabitha Babbitt's circular saw, they

claimed credit for the flat-sided broom, the common clothespin, a metal penpoint, cut nails, apple parer and corer, an automatic seed planter, a rotary or disc harrow, the screw propeller, brimstone matches, and a threshing machine. Most of their inventions were unpatented, because inventive inspiration was thought to derive from God and hence was not subject to monopoly. Some of the Shaker "inventions" were actually reinventions; the circular saw, for instance, is said to have been previously known in Europe. The Shakers did patent such inventions as a washing machine, a metal button for the base of tilting chairs, a folding pocket stereoscope, a counter-balanced window sash, and a chimney cap. Elijah Myrick invented the chimney cap at Harvard; a machine for sizing broom corn was also invented there.

Shaker ingenuity was not confined to strictly work-related activities. A Shirley Shaker, Abraham Whitney, devised a system of musical notation using letters instead of notes. Whitney was asked to visit Canterbury and Enfield, New Hampshire, to instruct believers in those communities.[7] The "Letteral system" was a distinctive feature of Shaker hymnals for many years.

These accomplishments were, of course, exceptional, but they grew out of the daily challenges confronting members as they attempted to "put their hands to work and hearts to God." Shaker journals are replete with entries cataloging the mundane daily tasks. One such journal kept by a Harvard Shaker woman in the mid-nineteenth century reflects how the sisters occupied themselves. The journal disjointedly lists the roster of Church Family ministry sisters and eldresses, office sisters and those assigned as "caire" sisters (nurses).

In addition, the journal records: "Jemima Blanchard, aged and most blind works at making seed bag, Eunice Wilds, care of the Brethren shirts, Anna Robbins, aged and feeble, works some in the weaving room. Hannah Babbitt, aged and most blind unable to do but little of anything. Tabitha Babbitt takes care of the boys footing, mittens, caps and spins. Elizabeth Myrick weaves makes frocks, Hannah Bridges makes shirts. Caroline King weaves. Hannah Blanchard works on sieves. Mary Robbins, nurse. Anna Orsment spins. Mary Chandler makes gowns."[8]

Each person was expected to share the burden of domestic chores and to promote commercial enterprises. The sisters did a steady business in the sale of maple sugar, jellies, pickles, and fancy goods. The men worked in their shops and did the heavy work in the fields. Villages became models of efficiency and order. Neighboring farmers, seeing the Shakers' luxuriant and well-groomed fields and learning of their abundant harvests, tried to copy their agricultural methods. One writer, William H. Dixon, commented that the granary was to the Shaker what the temple was to the Jew.[9] A measure of the Shaker skill as orchardists was the sale of applesauce at Shirley, said to total five or six tons annually.[10]

The brethren were constantly building new structures, renovating shops and dwellings, and embarking on village public works. A brick factory established in the town of Harvard in the 1840s supplied a source of building material more durable than wood. Shirley began using brick about the same time as Harvard, possibly from the same Burbank brick works that furnished brick for mills in Lancaster and Fitchburg. Harvard Shakers owned a stone quarry on Snake Hill in Groton.[11] There was a place in North Lancaster misnamed Shaker Quarry—so called because Shirley oxcarts were used to transport slate from the quarry to Boston for the roofs of the Old State House and the former Hancock House on Beacon Street. When the Hancock House was torn down, some of the slate was brought back and used to slate a barn in the Shaker settlement.[12] (Oxcarts were the chief means of transporting heavy loads prior to the coming of the railroad. The trip between Shirley and Boston took two days.[13])

Brick and stone buildings endured longest, of course, but certain wooden structures also proved long lasting. In the nineteenth century, the Square House was substantially renovated. The Shakers added a porch and applied new clapboards in 1805, and in 1845, they changed the roof style to gable.[14] (While making renovations, they found "a hollow passageway by the side of the chimney" which was Shadrack Ireland's old access from the cellar to the roof.[15])

Until mid-century, nearly every house had a well and a pump, some indoors. In 1855, when drought threatened their wells, Harvard Shakers were forced to build an ingenious water supply system. Far to the south of the village, at the base of Harvard's Oak Hill, there was a sparkling spring. Community members built an aqueduct running from the spring to a reservoir constructed on a hill behind the Square House. The pipeline extended 6,501 feet from the spring, which was at the 400-foot level, across the swamp, dipping to the 290-foot level, and thence to the reservoir at the 340-foot level. A slate stone marked each change in direction. The pipe had two valve gates leading to the village. The system was constructed at a cost of $5,000, the Shakers claimed.[16]

Another ambitious project involved building a stone channel for Bennett's Brook, which rises west of the Church Family buildings and flows north toward Ayer.

Ingenuity in water engineering also revealed itself by the hot water system in the cow barn. Elijah Myrick suspected that ice water was bad for the cows, so he had a steampipe run to the water trough in the cow yard. Shakers took good care of their herd of purebred Holsteins, and for good reason: milk and butter were village staples in the later years and also became lucrative marketable products. The tractor-like oxen deserved pampering, too, since they did the heavy work, including the winter snowplowing.

Perhaps the boldest venture in the Harvard-Shirley bishopric was attempted at Shirley: a cotton mill was built in 1849 for the manufacture of cloth and bedspreads. The mill, situated in the center of town, was of brick, one hundred and forty feet long and three stories high. Adjoining were four brick tenement houses for workers. The factory was called Shaker Mill, or Phoenix Mill, at first. The mill was dedicated on May 17, 1851, with more than 150 Shakers from Harvard and Shirley present.[17] The daylong ceremony, conducted by Elder William H. Wetherbee and Deacon Jonas Nutting, consisted of religious worship, marching, and song, and a dedicatory address by Lorenzo Dow Grosvenor of Harvard, whose long abstruse theological dissertation never mentioned the mill but rather was a belated refutation of a review of Benjamin Youngs's book *Testimony of Christ's Second Appearing*. Elder William Leonard also spoke.

The Shakers leased the mill to a New Bedford firm which

began operations in the spring of 1852, employing about one hundred persons (many of them immigrants, commonly known at the time as "foreigners").[18] The cotton mill was never a moneymaker for the Shakers, but the quality of workmanship evident in its construction, complete with tenement buildings, followed the Shakers' usual high standard.

Shakers insisted on simplicity in designing buildings and furniture, a style that contrasted with the Victorian ornateness and bric-a-brac clutter of the period. They anticipated by nearly a century the precept that form should follow function. Their houses of worship lacked cathedral pretensions; instead, the Shaker meeting house was a white clapboard rectangle with plain plaster walls admitting light through windows lacking stained glass. There were no altars with elaborate ceremonial paraphernalia, only benches which could be removed to permit marching over plain wooden floors. The same sense of simplicity guided the artisans who fashioned the familiar Shaker chairs. Furniture lacked contours, carvings and stencilwork, features which were considered useless and therefore of only superficial appeal.

The Shaker concept of beauty would come to be appreciated one day, but its ascetic simplicity was not initially popular. In fact, it was regarded as barren and ugly by many, among them Charles Dickens, who visited the New Lebanon village on his American tour in 1842. Dickens described a grim room with grim hats hung on grim pegs and a grim clock ticking the time away—grimly. He was otherwise disparaging in his comments, condemning "that bad spirit . . . which would strip life of its healthful graces, rob youth of its innocent pleasures, pluck from maturity and age their pleasant ornaments, and make existence but a narrow path towards the grave. . . ."[19]

The public generally shared Dickens' assessment of Shaker asceticism. What would happen, people asked, if young people were to fall in love? That concern was the theme of Nathaniel Hawthorne's short story "The Canterbury Pilgrims."

Romantic love did, in fact, invade the Shaker settlement occasionally.[20] At the end of the eighteenth century, Newcomb

Green and Gertrude Ochler, a young man and girl who had grown up in the Harvard village, fell in love and married with the blessing of the community. Newcomb had come to the Shakers as an infant, with his mother and sister Ellen. Newcomb's mother, Louisa Green, who had been deserted by her husband, had found happiness among the Shakers, first at Canaan, New York, and when Canaan closed in 1884, at Harvard. A Shaker upbringing provided security for her children.

After some years, an eleven-year-old girl named Gertrude Ochler was entrusted to Eldress Louisa's care. Gertrude had been left with the Shakers by her German immigrant father, who wanted to save her from the temper of his second wife. When Gertrude turned seventeen, she and Newcomb left the Shakers and were married; the Shakers gave them furniture for their house.[21]

The Shakers always claimed they held no one against their will. Couples in love were urged to test the genuineness of their devotion for a period of time before leaving; then they were presented household gifts or money to help their start in a new life. The Shakers contended that the training which young girls received was ideally suited to the roles of wife and mother, since they were taught "diligence, economy, and all branches of domestic knowledge."[22]

Not all love affairs progressed smoothly, as a Shaker journal entry of 1857 indicates: "Now comes sorrow to overflowing. Elder Sister and Bennet B take Lavinia to Harvard town to see Dr. Holman. He examined her and reports to Elder Sister that she is with child in a state of pregnancy. Thus Lavinia decides to go to the world and we accordingly pack her off. P.M. Bennett go and carry her to Brothers in Templeton. Henry concludes to follow being connected with her. Thus he is packed off also, no more to join our ranks. The ministry return to Harvard with akeing hearts."

Members guilty of indiscretions found that punishment could be uncompromising, and some seem to have been expelled from the Shaker community against their will. In 1875, Roxalana Grosvenor, who had served as an eldress in Harvard for four years, and her sister, Maria Fidelia, brought suit in Suffolk Court to recover for "services rendered to the defendant society, a religious community, commonly known as Shakers."[23] The plaintiffs maintained that they had been expelled from the society unjustly on August 1, 1869, and that they desired support for the period following their expulsion. The Grosvenor sisters asserted that they were expelled for alleged nonconformity to the beliefs and doctrines of the society, though they denied nonconformity.

The court found in favor of the defendant society, stating it could not determine whether or not the doctrines of the plaintiffs were consistent with the established belief of the society, but acknowledged that the ministry and elders had the power to expel members under their constitution. Compensation was denied.[24]

A Grosvenor brother, Augustus, makes a picturesque entry into Shaker history. As a Harvard elder, he was given the task of overseeing construction of a residence for the North Family. His enthusiasm exceeded his prudence, however, and the forty-room brick Rural Home left the society with a $25,000 debt when it was completed in 1853. The Harvard Shakers repaid the debt with the help of the Shirley Shakers, but Grosvenor—according to the account of Clara Endicott Sears—was disgraced, stripped of his title, and made to tend the swine. Overcome with humiliation—so goes the story—he died unexpectedly at the age of 57 on September 9, 1864. "Old Dr. McCollester (Dr. John Quincy McCollester) of Ayer was called," Miss Sears reported, "and owing to the excited clamoring of his friends an autopsy was held, and behold! his heart was rent in two. The heart was put into a jar and taken to the druggist's shop at Ayer, and there his friends reviewed it year by year and saw the rent fully three inches long that cleft it."[25]

Shaker villages, in the main, had distinguished leadership; Harvard and Shirley were no exception. William Leonard of Harvard is remembered as author of "A Discourse on the Order and Propriety of Divine Inspiration and Revelation," 1853, in which he expounded the rationale for the community economic order. Daniel Fraser of New Lebanon, who spent four years at Shirley; Elijah Myrick and Simon Atherton, of Harvard; and Shirley's John Whiteley were also competent writers and exponents of Shaker beliefs, whose reputations were based on talent, positive achievement, and long careers of leadership.

Elijah Myrick came to be respected well beyond the village circle. A gifted businessman, craftsman and spiritual leader, he served as an elder for seven years and as a trustee for forty years. He frequently acted in behalf of both the Harvard and Shirley societies, and sometimes in matters affecting the New Hampshire and Maine societies as well. Myrick served on the school board in the town of Harvard for ten years.

Most of Myrick's writings in the *Shaker Manifesto* were theological treatises—certainly dull reading by today's standards. But he sometimes demonstrated a surprisingly liberal attitude. When freethinker D. M. Bennett (who had once been a Shaker at New Lebanon, but later became a Bible-debunking skeptic) drew the wrath of the infamous censor Anthony Comstock and was charged with sending indecent literature through the mail, Myrick wrote a letter in Bennett's defense, deploring what he called the return of the inquisition. "It is not the 'faithful believers' that have advanced the world," he wrote. "History tells us it is the doubters—the 'infidels'—that the world owes the greatest debt of gratitude."[26]

Simon Atherton, a contemporary of Myrick's, served as Harvard trustee for fifty years. He was regarded as a wise and efficient manager, credited with building up the herb and seed industry. Atherton became a familiar figure on the streets of Boston, for he spent two days a week at the state capitol during the decades of his trusteeship looking after the community's business interests. He lodged at Boston's Quincy House for many years and was regarded as a regular boarder.[27]

The personalities of individuals like Myrick and Atherton are little revealed by Shaker records and photographs. Glimpses may be seen, however, in random recollections. One such concerns a Mullin family which owned property next to the Harvard Church Family during the Civil War. Mary Mullin, a widow, told this story, recounted a century later by a grandson.

Mrs. Mullin always kept a cow or two, which she was allowed to pasture with the Shakers' milking herd. The gate between the

Shaker property and hers was always supposed to be kept closed, but the Mullin boys left the gate open one time too many, and the Shakers' cows strayed into the Mullins' apple orchard. Apples had fallen on the ground and were fermenting; the cows feasted and became intoxicated. Simon Atherton descended with his hammer and spikes and indignantly told Mrs. Mullin, "Mary, I've warned you before. Now I'm going to spike the gate."

"Don't you do it," replied Mrs. Mullin, "for I'll only pull them out."

But while he was pounding in the spikes and she was arguing with him, one of the Mullin boys ran to tell Elder Elijah Myrick. The gate was spiked and Simon Atherton gone when Elder Elijah arrived.

Mrs. Mullin again threatened to pull the spikes, but Elder Elijah said only, "Patience, Mary, patience." Then he left. Elder Elijah wasn't gone long when up the path came Simon Atherton to pull the spikes.[28]

Myrick evidently well understood Atherton's volatile nature, which revealed itself on another occasion, as Shaker Marcia Bullard relates. One day, as Elder Simon was setting off for Boston, the head farmer told him that he needed some grass seed. Simon, who never spent money foolishly and lived by the adage, Take care of the pence and the pounds will take care of themselves, responded, "You don't need it and I won't get it!" The farmer turned to his help and said, "Boys, get your land ready, he says he will get it." "I didn't say I would get it, I said I *won't!*" Simon replied; but he reconsidered and got the seed.[29]

A teacher gives us a glimpse of Elijah Myrick during the time that he served on the town school board. Elijah made it a practice to visit the school every year to address the pupils and hear them recite. His address was always the same: "What we want, my dear children, is harmony—above all things harmony—harmony." He would seat himself, continue to mumble "harmony," and eventually doze off. The amused children would recite unmolested.[30]

The preeminent personage in the latter history of the Shirley community was John Whiteley. Circumstances that led Whitely to Shakerism and to eventual ascendancy over the Harvard–Shirley bishopric are fairly well documented. He was born in Huddersfield, England, in 1819, the year that marked the birth of Queen Victoria. (Whiteley once told a visitor that he was in Manchester on the day of Victoria's coronation and joined in a temperance prodession in her honor.[31]) Whitely learned about the Shakers in his youth, having heard social experimenter Robert Owen's description of the Shakers as successful communists. He immigrated to America in the summer of 1842, locating first in Newburgh, New York. The next year he took up a government section of eighty acres of land near Elgin, Illinois. He worked as a wool sorter there and in Dayton, Ohio for four years before he came down with "fever and the ague" and was advised to return East on doctor's orders. He obtained a position at a Lowell, Massachusetts woolen mill and settled in Andover.

Whiteley had heard about the scrupulous honesty of the Shakers when he first came to America. He tried without success at that time to learn more about the sect. A fellow workman in Lowell told Whiteley that he talked like a Shaker and should join them. The workman loaned Whiteley some doctrinal books about the Shakers, and Whiteley read these aloud with his wife during the winter evenings. Later, they made the acquaintance of a group of Shakers visiting friends in Andover. Whiteley and his wife accepted an invitation to visit the Shirley village, and were impressed by what they saw; they came back two months later, bringing their children with them, and took up residence with the South Family. The Whiteleys lived there for five years. Then John Whiteley was asked to take charge of the temporal affairs of the North Family. It was time for the Whiteleys to make a final commitment.

The couple—sweethearts since childhood—parted and gave up their children to the charge of the community. Although the children eventually left the Shakers, the father and mother were steadfast believers to the end of their lives. In a few years, Whiteley became elder of the North Family; then, on November 17, 1871, he was appointed to head the Harvard–Shirley ministry.

Whiteley took over the post held by Grove Babbitt Blanchard, who had served as elder for fifty years before failing health forced his retirement.[32]

In addition to his administrative ability and writings, Whiteley gained stature by the sheer appeal of his personality. He is described as "beloved by all" and "the soul of integrity"—as well as physically imposing, dignified and picturesque—"with long white hair, butternut-colored homespun trousers and coat made in a bygone fashion—and a very broad flat-brimmed hat."[33]

The strong personalities described here, and others like them, were to become a hallmark of the Shakers. At midcentury, it is plain that the ideas established by Shaker founders still evidenced themselves clearly in the characters of believers.

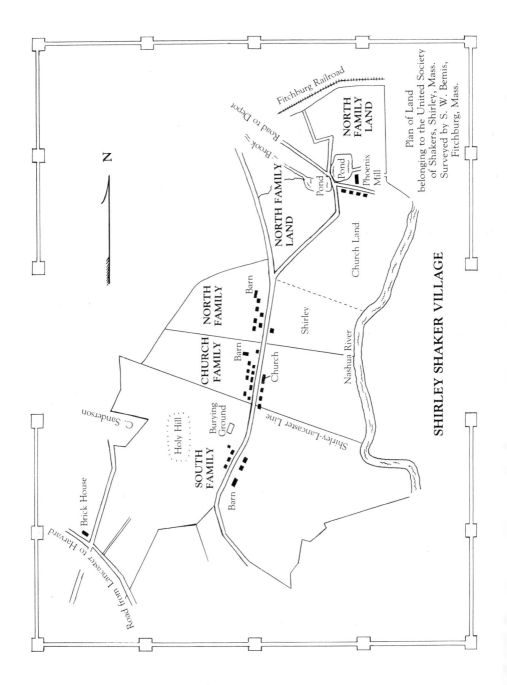

N

Plan of Land
belonging to the United Society
of Shakers, Shirley, Mass.
Surveyed by S. W. Bemis,
Fitchburg, Mass.

SHIRLEY SHAKER VILLAGE

Fitchburg Railroad

NORTH FAMILY LAND

Road to Depot

Brook

NORTH FAMILY LAND

Pond

Pond

Phoenix Mill

Church Land

NORTH FAMILY

Barn

Shirley

CHURCH FAMILY

Barn

Church

Nashua River

Shirley-Lancaster Line

C. Sanderson

Holy Hill

Burying Ground

SOUTH FAMILY

Barn

Brick House

Road from Lancaster to Harvard

8. Struggle and Decline

SHAKER LIFE IN HARVARD and Shirley continued in its familiar pattern during the latter part of the nineteenth century, but it was unmistakably an era of decline. Recruitment lagged, the Civil War took its toll, and the Shakers and their leaders were growing old.

In April 1858, a Shirley Shaker journal records the death and funeral of one of the sisters, concluding with the plaintive observation, "and so passeth away our Aged Friends. Our Family is growing less fast. More laborers are needed in the Lord's Vineyard. Send them, Lord, we pray. Thou alone canst help us."[1]

The Shirley village was visited in September 1858 by John Davis Long, preceptor of Westford Academy and subsequently governor of Massachusetts. Long observed the outward wealth of the village, but he also perceived a stagnation in its populace. "There were no young men, nor misses," he wrote in his journal. "All were either advanced in life or very young. I imagine there is not much inducement in their manner of life for hot-blooded lads and lasses to remain with them. Their children they obtain from alm-houses, etc."[2] Long attended a church service which he judged ludicrous, "but considering the neatness of everything pertaining to their kingdom, the marks of prosperity that were visible in their farms, their houses and trees, I thought their life was not altogether without its quiet pleasure."[3]

During the Civil War, Elder Frederick W. Evans visited President Abraham Lincoln in Washington to represent the pacifist view of the Shakers and to plead Shaker exemption as conscientious objectors. The president acceded to the request reluctantly, stating, "You ought to be made to fight; we need regiments of just such men as you."[4]

Until Lincoln's decision, the draft had caused the Shakers much grief. A notable case in Shirley was documented by Elder John Whiteley.[5] Three men assigned to the North Family, or Young Believers Order, were among a thirty-two man call-up in Massachusetts on July 17, 1863. Lorenzo D. Prouty and his brother, Nathan C. Prouty, and Horace S. Taber were ordered to report to Concord for induction, being furnished with passage for the short train ride. Upon reporting, the Proutys were exempted because their teeth were missing, but Brother Horace, although blind in one eye and of frail constitution otherwise, was accepted. Elder John, who accompanied the recruits to the examination, recorded that Brother Horace was given time to find a substitute, pay $300 in lieu of service, or report for duty. Taber anguished but did none of these, and on September 23 he was arrested at the Shaker village as a deserter. He was confined overnight in Concord, then transported to a guardhouse at a military camp on Long Island in Boston Harbor. Whiteley, then elder of the North Family, and bishopric ministry Elder Grove B. Blanchard visited him and interceded in his behalf with General Charles Devens and the post surgeon general, obtaining approval for a reexamination. The elders were told to gather documents certifying the previous poor health of the conscript. There followed anxious waiting and a barrage of solicitous correspondence between Shirley Shaker members and Brother Horace. Taber cataloged his tribulations: cold accommodations, the company of rough men who habitually swore and gambled, and the constant fear of being shipped South. Taber wrote that he would rather be shot. He received daily letters from Shirley urging him to keep up his courage and reminding him he was constantly in the prayers of his Shaker brethren.[6] Finally, thirty-three days after his arrest, he was allowed to return to the "good old Shirley" that he yearned for in his letters.

The Civil War was distressing to the Shakers for other reasons as well. Southern villages, while remaining neutral, were overrun by successive waves of Union and Confederate troops as the fortunes of war shifted. The Shakers tried to feed and billet the troops, but property was damaged and there was a general drain on resources. Northern villages also were affected, if only in the effort to divert revenue to assist the afflicted Southern markets for Shaker products.

There were intangible losses, too. In the words of Kentucky historian Thomas D. Clark, it was a cold and compromising age of materialism that followed the Civil War. The days of antebellum religious fervor and social experimentation were now history."[7]

In 1874, correspondent Charles Nordhoff visited fourteen Shaker societies, researching his book *The Communistic Societies of the United States*. He found that in Harvard and Shirley the ratio of women to men was even more disproportionate than in other communities. Harvard's ninety people included fifty-seven women and only seventeen men. Sixteen were children under 21, only four of those boys. The village employed sixteen or seventeen hired laborers.

Nordhoff counted only forty-eight residents in Shirley. Twelve were children—eight girls and four boys. Of the adults, six were men and thirty women. Nordhoff wrote, "Thirty-five years ago this society numbered 150 persons; twenty-four years ago, seventy-five; twenty years ago it had sixty. As the old people, the founders, died off, new members did not come in. They have not now many applications for membership, and of the children they adopt and bring up, not one in ten becomes a Shaker."[8]

Nordhoff said that the Shakers had nine or ten hired laborers—persons considered fortunate because the Shakers were kind and liberal in their dealings. However, the need to hire outside help constituted a drain on the village treasury. Shirley also had found it wise to sell its cotton mill because it ran them into debt, Nordhoff reported.

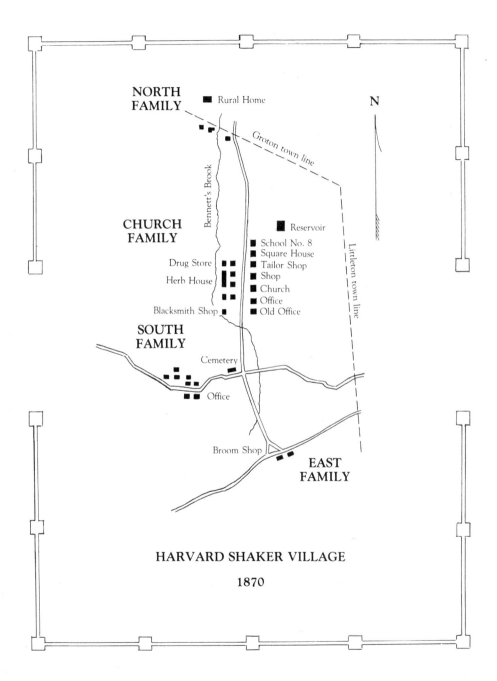

NORTH
FAMILY   ■ Rural Home   N

                                 ■

                          ■

                                    Groton town line

                  Bennett's Brook

CHURCH   ■ Reservoir
FAMILY   ■ School No. 8
                            ■ Square House   Littleton town line
          Drug Store ■ ■   ■ Tailor Shop
          Herb House ■ ■   ■ Shop
                      ■ ■   ■ Church
                            ■ Office
    Blacksmith Shop ■   ■ Old Office

SOUTH
FAMILY

                 Cemetery
          ■ ■
        ■ ■ ■
          ■ ■ Office

          Broom Shop ◊   ■ ■
                                      EAST
                                      FAMILY

HARVARD SHAKER VILLAGE

1870

113

Another visitor to the Shirley village was William Dean Howells, editor of the *Atlantic Monthly* and author of *The Rise of Silas
Lapham* and other notable works. During six weeks of the summer
of 1875, Howells stayed at a boardinghouse known as the "Brick
Tavern," a once notorious roadhouse on the Union Turnpike that
the Shakers had acquired both to accommodate guests and to elim-
inate a public nuisance. Howells studied the Shakers, shared in
their work, attended their services, and talked with their leaders.
He subsequently portrayed their lifestyle in such works as *The Un-
discovered Country*, *A Parting and a Meeting*, *Three Villages* and
The Day of Their Wedding.

Howells, whose father was Quaker, wrote a sympathetic article about the Shirley Shakers in the June 1876 issue of the *Atlantic
Monthly*. He told of attending several Sabbath services as well as
the funeral of a Shaker sister. He was impressed by the preaching
of elders John Whiteley and Daniel Fraser. He particularly enjoyed Fraser's talks, writing, "I always liked his speaking, for, if I
did not accept his Shakerism, I felt bound to accept his good sense;
and, besides, it is pleasant, after the generalizing of the pulpits, to
have the sins of one's fellow men frankly named and fully rebuked;
in this sort of satisfaction I sometimes almost felt without
reproach."[9]

Fraser had been a leading Shaker writer in New Lebanon for
decades before moving to Shirley to serve as elder of the North
Family, a transfer probably made to fill the leadership vacuum oc-
curring upon Elder Grove Blanchard's incapacitation and John
Whiteley's promotion. Fraser and Whiteley impressed Howells
both because of their sanctity and because of their literary worldliness. He remarked that both were readers of most of the late books
of religious controversy. He specifically applauded their exposure
to two of his contemporaries, Mark Twain and Bret Harte, whose
careers Howells helped to promote.

Unlike Dickens, Howells was not repelled by Shaker accommodations. "The first impression of all," he wrote, "is cleanliness,
with a suggestion of barrenness which is not inconsistent, however, with comfort, and which comes chiefly from the aspect of
the unpapeied walls, the scrubbed floors hidden only by rugs and

strips of carpeting, and, the plain flat finish of the woodwork."[10] He described Shaker Sabbath marching as thrilling and fantastic, but not ludicrous.

There is, however, one poignant passage in the Howells description. A married sister of one of the Shakers happened to visit with her baby. The infant was gathered into the lap of one of the Shaker brothers while Shaker sisters flocked admiringly around the child. The mother stood outside the group while the sisters doted on her offspring. Commented Howells, "Somehow the sight was pathetic. If she were right and they were wrong, how much of heaven they had lost in renouncing the supreme good of earth!"[11]

The Shirley Shakers were delighted in having such a distinguished guest as Howells among them and treasured an autographed photograph he gave them, but Shaker critics considered his writings an oversimplified, sentimental and ambivalent commentary on Shaker life.

The procession of visitors at the Shaker villages was constant.[12] The visitors, many of them the leading social commentators, journalists and authors of the day, had mixed reactions, frequently applauding village economy while remaining skeptical, noncommittal, or even hostile on matters of morality and lifestyle.

Our perception of Shaker life owes much to the accounts of visitors, but a more intimate view comes from an insider, Arthur T. West, who lived among the Harvard Shakers as a boy from 1884 to 1889 and returned to teach in the Shaker school in 1896 and 1897.[13] As an educated lay person well acquainted with Elijah Myrick, Simon Atherton, and others, West brought a unique perspective to his reminiscences, which he summarized in an article in the *New England Quarterly*.

West outlined a typical Shaker day, in which rising and retiring and work and meals were regimented by the tolling of a bell. The day commenced at four-thirty in the morning, with chores until five-fifty, breakfast at six, work until eleven-thirty—when a bell would summon men from the fields for the noon meal—back to work in the afternoon, supper at six, a period of relaxation, and lights out at nine.

West worked in the brethren's shop making brooms and pack-aging herbs or in the fields behind the ox teams. He also was fre-quently assigned to help octogenarian Ezra Newton at the task of weaving door mats from corn husks. West wrote warmly of his childhood experiences and was sympathetic in describing Shaker beliefs and manner of worship.

West wrote that quiet—an extra stillness—pervaded the vil-lage on the Sabbath, commencing at 4:00 p.m. on Saturday and ending at 4:00 p.m. on Sunday. Sunday meeting was at 10:00 a.m. Before the service, the brothers and sisters assembled in the bell-house, where they visited quietly. At the tolling of the bell, they filed out of the building, crossed the road, and approached the meeting house entrances by separate walkways, the brothers en-tering at the left and the sisters at the right. Once assembled in-side, they stood silently in ranks until a sister began a song, in which they would all join. An elder would make a few remarks, there would be another song, and an eldress would speak.

"Suddenly a change comes over the gathering," West wrote. "A march song is started. The ranks of the brothers and sisters break. The elders cross the room as the rest of the brothers fall in, forming a double line. The sisters start forward, and almost as if by magic the assembly is marching around the room in double lines, singing their march song, keeping time with their hands and with a very slight upward spring to each step. By a previous ar-rangement four sisters and a brother form a hollow square in the center of the room. These are selected for their vocal qualifications and they lead in the singing."[14]

West witnessed the spectacle of a sister spinning like a top for several minutes without getting dizzy. He also observed members who exhibited trembling, or shaking, of the entire body. "There were, it is true," he wrote, "some things done during their hour of worship which to those of the world might seem a bit queer, and accounts of these demonstrations have been seriously enlarged upon by those who did not understand . . . there was never any shouting or weird motions, such as throwing oneself on the floor, or any confusion in the ranks of the sisters or brothers."[15]

Both West and Howells observed that there were never any audible prayers, although silent prayers were offered at mealtimes and also before retiring at night. Howells said that the monastic rule of silence was observed at meals because there would be too great confusion if all talked together. The status of prayer in the Shaker belief was once explained by Elder Henry Blinn of Canterbury, who said that the Shakers accepted as their guide the admonition of Jesus: "Do not sound a trumpet before thee . . . when thou prayest thou should not be as the hypocrites are, for they love to pray standing in the synagogues and in the corners of the streets, that they may be seen of men."[16]

Howells and West both noted the peculiarity of Shaker dress which, while not a unique uniform, was dictated by use rather than vanity, and reflected a style prevalent at the time of the society's founding. Women wore either lace caps or deep, straw bonnets which concealed the cheeks in profile, a kerchief draped over the shoulders and bosom, a dress of ankle length with heavy pleating of the skirt. Material was usually wool, linen or calico, depending on the season and occupation of the wearer. Men usually wore their hair long in the back and cut square across the forehead. Outer garments included trousers, a frock of knee length and shoes of heavy leather. Both sexes wore collars. Men often wore wide-brimmed felt hats. Colors tended to be drab brown, blue, and gray. Shakers looked increasingly odd as the decades passed.

Shakers tried to become progressive in maintaining communication with the world and among believers, especially during Elder Frederick Evans's time. A society periodical was established in 1871. It lasted twenty-eight years and was successively titled *The Shaker*, *The Shaker and Shakeress*, *The Shaker Manifesto*, and *The Manifesto*. Daniel Fraser, John Whiteley, and Elijah Myrick wrote frequent theological articles for its pages. Many such articles were tedious, but the magazine also had interesting reprints from the secular press, tidbits of community gossip, and always fascinating obituaries, which—in the absence of births and marriages—were the most vital statistics they had. The Shakers seemed to adopt the sensationalized headline style of the day, using such attention-getters as "Is Woman a Slave?" "Twelve Reasons Why No Rational Being Should Use Tobacco," "Bisexuality of God," and "Cheap Food For the Starving." The periodical took its place with the Bible and Shaker-authored books as staple reading matter in the villages.

The Millennial Laws, which were "revised and reestablished" in 1860, regulated the Shakers' contact with worldly publications: [17]

"Brethren and sisters are not allowed to purchase or borrow books of the world or other families of believers without permission of the Elders of the family wherein they live.

"No one should read books, when out among the world that are not allowed of among Believers. If the world should offer any Believer a book which would be allowed of, though they might not have had liberty to get such a book, it would be better to receive it than to give offence, but it should be shown to the Elders before it is read or circulated.

"No books or pamphlets of any kind are allowed to be brought into the family without the knowledge and approbation of the Elders, except on conditions as before shown."

The Millennial Laws forbade correspondence which did not pass inspection of the elders:

"If any member of the family should receive a letter from any person, or persons, such person receiving the letter must show it to the Elders before it is opened, and it should be opened and read in their presence.

"If any member should write a letter to send abroad, (i.e., outside the community), it must be shown to the Elders before it is sealed or sent away. But the office deacons are allowed to write or receive letters on temporal business without showing them to the Elders."

Millennial Laws also governed the availability of newspapers: "Newspapers shall be received alone by those at the Office, or outer court, and should there be returned and kept when they have been perused in the family; and none should come into the family except by the knowledge of the Elders."

Arthur West stated that "magazines, novels or newspapers were unknown among the [Harvard] Shakers and were found only at the office in the Church Family for the use of elders and trustees."[18] Charles Nordhoff commented that Harvard's Shakers had a small library and subscribed to a great many newspapers, but "do not let books interfere with work."[19] Shirley had plenty of books and newspapers, but no regular library, Nordhoff said.[20]

The Shakers used the Lancastrian method of education, a monitorial system of instruction in which advanced pupils taught pupils below them. Nordhoff was impressed by his visit to the Shirley school, where "physiology was taught, and with remarkable success as it seemed to me, with the help of charts; the children seemed uncommonly intelligent and bright. The school is open three months in the summer and three in the winter—two hours in the forenoon and two in the afternoon; and the teacher, a young girl, was also caretaker of the girls. Singing school is held, for the children, in the evening."[21]

Nordhoff asked the sisters if the Shakers liked to take children. An eldress replied, "Yes, we like to take children—but we don't like to take monkeys." According to Nordhoff, the Shakers had discovered that "blood will tell," and it was better to take children of religious parents than otherwise.[22]

Though the Shaker schools maintained high standards, they were sometimes in conflict with civil authorities. Horace Mann, secretary of the Massachusetts Board of Education and credited as the father of public schooling in the United States, had clashed with the Harvard and Shirley Shakers in the early 1840s when they refused to accept supervision and inspection by local school authorities. Mann was largely responsible for the secularization of public schools and for laws which prohibited sectarian schoolbooks. He warned the Shakers in his fifth annual report to the State Board of Education that their resistance could lead to consequences much more serious than they supposed. Mann expressed alarm lest the example of the Shakers be followed in other towns where there was a diversity of creeds.[23] The Shakers maintained that their beliefs were different from the rest of the world, and they wished their schools to be separate and entirely under their own control.

In later years this conflict did not prevent Elijah Myrick from being elected to the School Committee in Harvard or John Whiteley to the same post in Shirley. The Shaker school was favorably rated in the annual report of the School Committee for the school year 1881-82—when Myrick was chairman—as follows: "Miss

Mary Kelley taught this school during the spring and fall terms. Miss Kelley carries with her an earnestness and force of character that compels the respect and attention of her pupils. Her success has been complete, bringing her school well up toward the front rank. Miss Kelley commenced the winter term, but was obliged to withdraw on account of ill health, much to the regret of the community and friends of the school. Her place was acceptably filled by Miss Marcia Bullard, a teacher of large experience."[24]

There remained, however, some Shaker suspicion of interference with its school. In 1896, a *Boston Globe* article quotes Elder John Whiteley as stating, "The town declines to support a school for us on the ground of its being sectarian, and our children in the Shaker dress and manners cannot be subjected to the jeers and scoffs of the pupils of the common schools and come in contact with all that a school child must."[25]

The Shakers elected to support their own schools in order to maintain them free of secular influences. Non-Shaker parents often sent their children, testifying to the favorable esteem in which Shaker schools were held. The towns were content to be free of the burden, and there seemed to be a good reciprocal relationship between the civil and Shaker authorities in the townships.

Indeed, while the Shakers were always careful to preserve the distinctive quality of their communities, contacts with their neighbors were frequent and varied.

Arthur West, for instance, told of a field trip he arranged for his pupils. West proposed that his charges, a group of girls, attend an evening lecture sponsored in town. He first appealed to his aunt, Family Eldress Annie Walker. Obtaining her blessing, he approached the ministry eldresses, Eliza Babbitt and Maria Foster. The whole idea sounded very un-Shakerlike, and Eldress Eliza—who was over ninety at the time—said nay to the proposal. But West was persistent. He said the girls would be properly chaperoned, seats would be reserved for them at the lecture hall, Brother Frank Stanton would drive the barge, and Eldress Annie would guarantee their safe return. West's assurances won over Eldress Maria. Finally, Eldress Eliza relented. On the night of the lecture, the girls were in attendance, accompanied by no less than Eldress Maria. Shakers regularly attended the lecture series thereafter.[26]

West's reminiscences of his years with the Shakers also included the story of Sister Susanna MacGooden, a witty Irish Shaker who was nearly as round as she was tall. One day as she was crossing the village road, a carriage drew up with four very proper-looking tourists aboard. One of them addressed the sister, stating, "We are from Boston, and we have come out to see some of the Shaker curiosities." Sister Susanna, over ninety at the time, did a slow pirouette and replied, "Well, take a good look at me. I'm one of the Shaker curiosities."[27]

Persons from all classes of society sought out the Shakers, including a legion of tramps and hoboes who capitalized on the Shakers' sense of hospitality. (Elder Daniel Fraser once told William Dean Howells that some of these knights of the open road looked as if the pit had vomited them up.) One such derelict gentleman visited the South Family one frosty morning in search of nourishment. Sister Catherine obliged with servings of fried apples, dark bread, milk and apple pie. Since the visitor's shoes were quite shabby, Sister Catherine dug out a pair of Shaker boots and gave them to him. He accepted the gift with profuse thanks and departed. Later, the new boots were found parked upon a nearby stone wall, the visitor preferring, apparently, the comfort and ventilation of his old footwear.[28]

Elder Whiteley attracted a procession of visitors, including Dr. Samuel A. Green of Groton, one-time Boston mayor, who used to call upon the Shirley society every Fourth of July in his retirement years. Green dined with Elder John and the sisters. The ex-mayor told people it was the only quiet spot he could find on that day.[29]

The Shakers had become good neighbors and were known to help out in times of crisis. During the potato famine in Ireland, they sent money to help feed the starving. The Harvard community earned the affection of their neighbors in Ayer when a fire destroyed more than thirty buildings, including the Unitarian

Church, on the night of Saturday, April 13, 1872. The newly incorporated town, formerly known as Groton Junction, sustained a net loss over and above insurance of $100,000. Thirty families were rendered homeless. "A relief committee was appointed to solicit aid," a historian wrote. "The several families of the neighboring Harvard Shakers were among the first to offer aid by sending money and provisions, and by cancelling bills due them from parties who suffered loss by the fire.[30]

The following year, when forest fires around Ayer's Sandy Pond kept firefighters laboring day and night for weeks, Elder Elijah dispatched several brothers each day to help. The Fire Engineers, in their annual report, expressed gratitude for the free contribution, noting that the natural tendency of some in such cases takes the form of a raid on the town treasury.

The Harvard Shakers experienced their own fire disaster on September 20, 1894, when flames swept through the so-called Great Barn, ox barn, tanning house and icehouse, causing at least $10,000 damage and destroying the winter supply of hay and vegetables. A Shaker diarist[31] detailed the loss as including some 100 tons of new hay, 300 bushels of potatoes, a large lot of beans, some herbs, 15,000 gallons of vinegar, a quantity of cider, and other provisions. Careless smoking was listed as the cause. At the time it was built, the Great Barn was reputed the largest in the state. Dimensions of the large barn were listed as 140 by 80 feet—a width perhaps exaggerated by a separately constructed addition. The ox barn measured 80 by 40 feet.

The barn at Shirley, which would also eventually fall victim to fire, was smaller than the Harvard barn, measuring 120 by 42 feet. A guest of Elder John Whiteley reported in 1889 that the barn housed a herd of about forty Guernseys, Jerseys, and Ayrshires. The community had a hay crop that year of from 150 to 200 tons. "The loads of hay," he wrote, "are driven in at the upper part of the barn, the hay thrown off down the sides, the team having space at the front end to be turned and then driven out at the entrance. They have beautiful apple orchards;" the visitor wrote, "last year they gathered 1,000 barrels."[32] Another guest recounted that cobwebs were "unknown to the barn."[33]

Shaker longevity was legendary. In the decade of the 1880s, the average age of death at Harvard was slightly more than seventy, a mortality rate that society in general would not equal for almost a century. Nordhoff noted the superior health of Shakers in almost all the villages he visited. New Lebanon Elder Giles Avery credited the sexless existence in an article entitled "Longevity of Virgin Celibates." Elder Frederick Evans estimated that abstinence added ten years to the average life span.

The Harvard Shakers attributed some of their longevity to the community's drinking water. This literal fountain of youth had been introduced in 1855 when drought caused the supply of well water to fail and the Shakers laid an aqueduct to a spring one mile away. Thereafter, all the water drunk by the community came from this spring, resulting, they claimed, in a sixteen percent improvement in the rate of longevity (comparing the death records of 1835–1855 and 1860–1880).

When the Shaker medicinal spring water began to be sold commercially, Elijah Myrick and several other residents testified to its effects on their health. Stated Elder Elijah in 1881, "I am one of the youngest of a family, seven of which died of scrofulous consumption. All but one died prior to the introduction of the spring water; and I was pronounced 'a sure victim of the fatal disease.'

"I was seldom free from scrofula [tubercular lymphatic disease] in some of its forms—boils, sores and swollen joints, with a constant dry cough.

"At the time unconscious that it was the water that was affecting me, my humors gradually left me, and the swellings and cough ceased. And for more than twenty years I have not had a symptom of the disease; and am free to say that my present health, and freedom from any tendency to the return of the disease, is due to the water, as a blood purifier."[34]

A testimonial was also elicited from the Massachusetts assayer, and turbidity figures were quoted to show that the chemical content of the water exceeded in purity that of the famous Poland Spring mineral water.

Unfortunately, neither a fountain of youth nor a celibate regimen could keep the Shakers alive forever; second and third generations of Shakers were disappearing from the scene. Deaths included Elders Grove Blanchard and Thomas Hammond in 1880 at ages 83 and 80 respectively; Olive Chandler, who had so much impressed the Transcendentalists Alcott and Lane, in 1887 at age 73; Simon Atherton in 1888 at age 85; and Mary Robbins in 1889 at age 89.

Elder Elijah Myrick died on February 9, 1890, at age sixty-six; his death was mourned both within the Shaker village and the Harvard community at large. He was the last remaining of the twelve Myrick children who had been brought into the community. Myrick's passing culminated a decade in which Shaker leadership in the Harvard–Shirley bishopric was decimated.

(Elder Elijah took one secret with him to the grave. When the order went out from the central ministry to dispose of the Fountain Stones once used at the outside worship ground to save them from possible desecration, Myrick buried the Holy Hill tablet somewhere in the village.[35])

Death also claimed Elder Frederick Evans on March 6, 1893, in his eighty-fifth year. He had been chief spokesman for the Shakers for more than three decades, presiding over a shrinking society.[36] Elder Frederick had been considered liberal, worldly and tolerant and was blamed by some Shakers for policies that contributed to decline. Elder Harvey L. Eads of South Union, Kentucky, and Elder Henry C. Blinn of Canterbury, New Hampshire, were among those who were critical, Blinn referring derisively to "the Gospel according to St. Frederick."[37]

In explaining the Shaker decline to correspondent Nordhoff, Evans cited such causes as overinvestment in land, a shift in emphasis from agriculture to manufacturing, and substitution of worldly products for Shaker-made goods. "We used to have more looms than now," Evans said, "but cloth is sold so cheaply that we gradually began to buy. It is a mistake; we buy more cheaply than we can make, but our home-made cloth is much better than we can buy; and we have now to make three pair of trousers, for instance, where before we made one. Thus our little looms would even now be more profitable—to say nothing of the independence we secure in working them."[38]

The matriarchal succession underwent considerable juggling as the ranks of the aging sisterhood began to thin drastically. Eldress Maria Foster "took the flight of the spirit," as the Shakers expressed it, in 1897, and Marcia Bullard died in 1899; both were 76 when they died. Eldress Eliza Babbitt, who was a Shaker for eighty years, forty of them as a member of the ministry, and had acquired a reputation for unusual sagacity during twenty-eight years as superior eldress, died in February 1900 at 94.

The time had arrived when even the eldest Shaker no longer had as much as a secondhand recollection of Mother Ann. Even Ezra Beaman Newton, who was born in Paxton, Massachusetts on February 24, 1795 and lived until April 23, 1896, lacked personal contact with Mother Ann or her younger contemporaries. Newton was 53 years old before he became a Shaker in 1848, on the rebound from the Millerite movement. He parted amicably from his wife, stipulating that the couple's two children not be taken from her. Brother Ezra was a zealous Shaker for the rest of his life, which was protracted beyond Ezra's expectations—and his hopes.

When advanced age rendered it necessary, Sister Catherine Walker cared for him. She died after several years, but, before she did, she told Brother Ezra, "Now be patient and wait until you have passed your one hundreth birthday and then, if it be possible, I will come for you."[39] Brother Ezra mourned Sister Catherine's passing but was comforted by her promise.

Brother Ezra's centennial birthday was the occasion for a major celebration. Five reporters showed up at Harvard's South Family where Brother Ezra made his home. Elder John Whiteley presided as a large number of friends and neighbors from Ayer, Harvard and Shirley gathered, along with twenty-six of Brother Ezra's relatives.

The Shakers also observed Brother Ezra's 101st birthday, after which he lapsed into poor health. He frequently remarked that he wanted to die with the sunrise, and, according to a newspaper obituary, "It was just as the sun was rising over the hills that death claimed him and immediately there was joy in the Shaker settlement to know a good man had departed just as he desired to."[40]

Brother Ezra's corpse was washed with whiskey and placed in

a cool place where it would keep for the public funeral. John Whiteley presided and delivered the eulogy. Other testimonials were rendered by Maria Foster, Ellen Green, Stephen McKnight, Marcia Bullard, Mary Ann Whiteley, Johanna Randall, Annie Walker and Myra McLean. Brother Ezra's coffin was then placed on a wagon and taken to the Shaker burial ground.[41]

Brother Ezra's death coincided with the breakup of the Harvard South Family, as shrinking membership forced consolidation of community property. In 1890, the Harvard Shakers had sold their East Family property, consisting of two houses, a large barn, and 100 acres of land.[42]

The Rural Home of the North Family was leased for private uses, first as a summer boarding house and then as a sanitarium.

Arthur West closed his school in the Harvard community in June of 1898. A Shaker diarist noted that the children were saddened.

In 1899, buildings at the discarded South Family were sold to a newly married couple, Fred and Dora Avery, who were wed in a ceremony at the Rural Home.

An early handbill described the attractions of the resort at the Rural Home. John H. Sprague, a Civil War veteran, was listed as manager, and he promoted the site as a country summer resort "only an hour's ride from Boston via Fitchburg Railroad; eight trains each way daily." Guests were offered free use of the "Celebrated Mineral Spring."[43]

A Harvard correspondent for the *Manifesto*, after noting the failure of the 1897 apple crop, reported, "We have leased our Rural Home to Dr. Watkins for a sanitarium, and he is now putting in the necessary appliances."[44]

Dr. Charles E. Watkins, listing himself as physician in charge with Jay Chaapel as superintendent, billed the Rural Health Home, as he called it, as a place "where diseases are cured without medicines." The Watkins handbill stated that the three-and-one-half-story brick structure was "built in the most substantial manner, thirty rooms, large, convenient and sunny with wide halls; long lines of maple trees border both sides of the street, and the neat, cheerful atmosphere of Shaker Village is our nearest neighbor."[45]

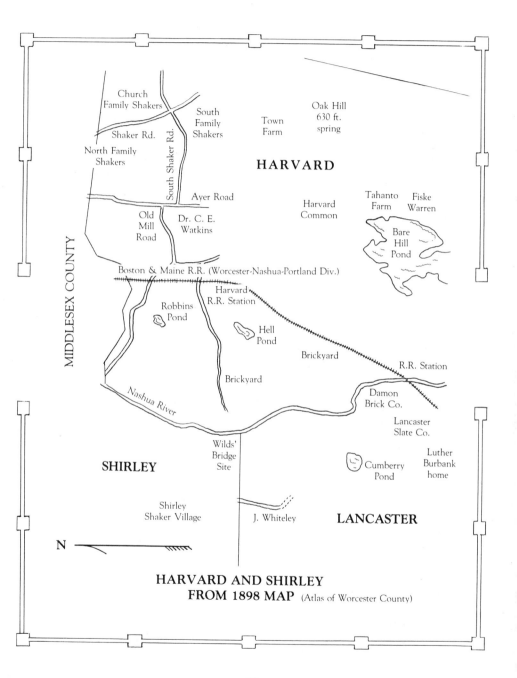

Church
Family Shakers

South
Family
Shakers

Town
Farm

Oak Hill
630 ft.
spring

Shaker Rd.

South Shaker Rd.

North Family
Shakers

HARVARD

Ayer Road

Old
Mill
Road

Dr. C. E.
Watkins

Harvard
Common

Tahanto
Farm

Fiske
Warren

Bare
Hill
Pond

MIDDLESEX COUNTY

Boston & Maine R.R. (Worcester-Nashua-Portland Div.)

Harvard
R.R. Station

Robbins
Pond

Hell
Pond

Brickyard

R.R. Station

Brickyard

Nashua River

Damon
Brick Co.

Lancaster
Slate Co.

Wilds'
Bridge
Site

SHIRLEY

Cumberry
Pond

Luther
Burbank
home

Shirley
Shaker Village

J. Whiteley

LANCASTER

N

**HARVARD AND SHIRLEY
FROM 1898 MAP** (Atlas of Worcester County)

127

The Harvard–Shirley bishopric was falling into a pattern of decline that had forced the closing of other Shaker communities, including Tyringham, Massachusetts, which dissolved in 1875; Groveland, New York, which was sold in 1895; and North Union, Ohio, which dissolved in 1889.

John Whiteley, in a letter to New Lebanon Elder Joseph Holden, dated June 26, 1889, had written, " . . . am sorry to hear of the loss of Groveland and to hear that North Union must be broken up—The question very naturally arises—Which society next? I hope sincerely *not Shirley.*"[46]

In fact, the Shirley Shakers were also retrenching. The mill was now owned and operated by the Samson Cordage Company (whose trademark, registered July 4, 1884, is claimed as the oldest in America). In 1900, the brick dwelling of the Shirley South Family, which once had housed thirty-two people, was razed.[47]

John Whiteley was to be the last patriarch in the ministry of Harvard and Shirley, a towering successor to the three previous superior elders—Eleazer Rand, John Warner, and Grove Blanchard.

Whiteley was worldly-wise and respected. A *Boston Globe* correspondent wrote of him, "Of the many who daily drive up to the little post office at Shirley village, receive their portions of mail, exchange greetings, discuss the signs of the times, etc. there is none more conspicuous than 'Elder John,' as he is familiarly addressed by all who meet him on common ground."[48]

Elder John was over eighty as the nineteenth century ended, but his pace never slackened. His responsibilities were many. On August 19, 1900 he wrote to the central ministry with a note of weariness in his words: "Dr. Watkins has left the Rural Home—so that is on our hands again." An advertisement subsequently appeared offering "this well known place, formerly a Shaker Home" for let or lease—inquiries to "John Whiteley, Trustee." In September a destructive gale blew down half of the north elm at the Elijah Wilds house. Whiteley notes in his diary: "Spend the strength left me on the big elm—trimming the limbs to some extent." Whiteley continued to make trips into Boston at least weekly, conducting business and often staying overnight at the Crawford

JOHN WHITELEY,

DEALER IN

PRESSED AND SWEET HERBS,

Hops, Rose-Water, Shaker Brooms, ,

DISH-MOPS, FLOOR-MOPS, &C., &C.

P. O. ADDRESSES:

AYER, MASS.. ··AND·· SHIRLEY VILLAGE, MAS ·

Elder John Whiteley (above), and his business card.
(Courtesy of Elmer R. Pearson)

Eldress Annie Walker (top left) *(Courtesy of Ralph Richardson)*

Eldress Catherine B. Walker (top right) *(Courtesy of Ralph Richardson)*

Arthur T. West *(Courtesy of Lillian West)*

"Oldest and youngest Shaker. Ezra Newton 101 Years." The inscription on this old photograph marks the birthday celebration of Brother Ezra, who is posed with other Shakers and probably relatives. Eldress Annie Walker is at right. (Courtesy of Barbara MacKenna)

Eldress Louisa Green
(Courtesy of Ann Callahan)

Eldress Ellen Green
(Courtesy of Ray Farrar)

Four generations of Greens. Eldress Louisa Green; her son, Newcomb, at right; Rubert Green, her grandson, at left; and infant Gertrude Green, Rubert's first child. The child was born July 10, 1913. (Courtesy of Connie Thayer)

Sister Annie Belle Tuttle (Courtesy of Fruitlands Museums)

Mrs. Dora Avery befriended the Shakers. (Courtesy of Connie Thayer)

These three sisters were together at the closing of both Harvard and Shirley. From left, Eldress Josephine C. Jilson, Sister Annie Belle Tuttle, and Sister Laura Beal. (Courtesy of the Western Reserve Historical Society)

Eldress Josephine Jilson (Courtesy of Fruitlands Museums)

Sister Olive Hatch, who lived to be 100. (Courtesy of the Harvard Historical Society)

Frank Stanton (top right) *and Frankie Hobbs* (lower right) *became boyhood friends after being taken in at the Harvard Shaker Village. Frankie's older sister, Edith* (above), *visited him often and joined in his friendship with Stanton. The frail Hobbs boy died in his teens, but Stanton and Edith Hobbs were married. (Courtesy of Grace [Stanton] Ingerson)*

Myra McLean (Courtesy of Ray Farrar)

*Sister Lottie Tremper
(Courtesy of Ray Farrar)*

Fiske Warren, who bought the Harvard Shaker property. (Courtesy of Mrs. Charles Perkins)

House or the Parker House. Diary entries for one month place him in Boston four times, Worcester and Fitchburg twice, and Roxbury once, along with frequent shuttles to Harvard and into Shirley village. On days spent within the Shaker community, Elder John worked for hours in the mop shop. He directed the sale of various real estate holdings, including the Brick Tavern, various woodlots, and Shaker holdings in Lancaster and Shirley at Spec and Fort Ponds.[49]

On January 1, 1901, Elder John noted in his diary the start of a new year and a new century: "What may it not bring to us in many ways."

9. The Closing
of Harvard and Shirley

WHAT MAY IT NOT BRING to us in many ways . . ." The
twentieth century brought rapid changes in a world which was to
encroach more and more upon the Shaker communities. Faced
with a continued decline in their population and independence,
the Shakers were eventually forced to a sad decision: the settlements in Harvard and Shirley were sold.

A non-Shaker couple had owned the buildings of the South
Family since 1899. Fred Avery was a farmer from Enfield, New
Hampshire, where he had known the Shakers, and was several
years senior to his bride, a woman of pioneering Ohio stock. The
vivacious Dora Avery quickly became a confidante of the Shakers
as well as an appreciative student of their domestic arts. Much of
what is known about the Harvard Shakers in the early 1900s is
owed to her recollections.

Daily life among the Shakers, even during the period of
retrenchment and decline, was far from grim; in fact, Shakers
seemed to have had as much fun as other Americans did in that
era. It was an exciting time in the nation's history, and the
Shakers, by reason of their constant travel and interchange with

each other and with the world's people, were neither isolated nor lonely. The Shakers often went in groups to Walden Pond in Concord and to Lake Whalom near Leominster to participate in meetings of the Women's Christian Temperance Union and other activities. On more than one occasion, a group of the popular Canterbury Shaker musicians came to call. The local newspaper, in recording one such visit by the sextet of two brothers and four sisters, commented that they performed "from a repertory so entirely unique and original as to be a continual surprise. Such a concert is well worth going many miles to hear . . ."[1]

The Shakers joined with their fellow Americans in the new fascination with the automobile. In 1905, this item appeared: "Two young men from Boston, with their automobiles, were at the Shakers recently, and took 15 of the Shaker sisters at different times on automobile rides."[2]

The young century brought other technological wonders that seemed to herald a golden age. Electricity made its local debut. Shirley was lighted by electric light in 1904, causing "much favorable comment throughout the town."[3] Harvard was later in becoming electrified. The Ayer newspaper reported on November 23, 1912: "Harvard can now light up with electricity, the current being turned on Wednesday night for the first time. Many of the houses, including the town hall and store are lighted, and several more residences are in process of wiring."

The Shakers enjoyed life's simple pleasures: playing checkers, dominoes, and other games, staging entertainments such as Bible scenes, doing puzzles, playing croquet, cooking chestnuts, fishing, going on hikes in the woods, taking sleigh rides in the winter, coasting, and holding popcorn parties. The observance of Christmas—at least in the latter years—paralleled celebrations by the world's people. Commented the local news correspondent, "At the Harvard Shakers Christmas service [1901] was held on Christmas night, chorus singing and readings by the younger members of the society made a very pleasant hour. Recitation by Master Frank Hobbs was especially well rendered. The entertainment was given in the main dining hall which was draped with strings of evergreen while in the center stood a tree with presents for everyone."[4] Of the 1903 observance, it was reported, "The young people of the Harvard Shakers gave an entertainment to the older sisters on Thursday evening. The long dining room was tastily decorated with evergreen and laurel and the tree bore a token of remembrance for each one. B.J. Goss [Bliss Goss, foreman of the hired men] collected the laurel for the occasion . . . ."[5]

The Shakers maintained an active interest in current events. When President William McKinley was assassinated in 1901, eleven persons from the Harvard bishopric attended the funeral, including Bliss Goss, Stephen McKnight, Louisa Green, Lottie Tremper, Sadie Maynard, Nathaniel Nilant and Frank Stanton.[6] Four years later, Eldresses Annie Walker from the Harvard community and Josephine C. Jilson from Shirley attended the Shaker Peace Conference staged at Mount Lebanon on August 31, 1905.[7] This assemblage of scholars was billed by the Shakers as rivaling the peace convention President Theodore Roosevelt had arranged at Wentworth-by-the-Sea in Portsmouth, New Hampshire (which resulted in the signing of a treaty on September 5, ending the Russo-Japanese War).

Many people visited the Shakers and made purchases at their stores; Harvard and Shirley both sold peppermints, which were very popular. Clara Endicott Sears reported being at the store one day while Eldress Annie Walker waited on a woman and her young daughter at the confectionery counter. The girl was a very pretty child, and Eldress Annie came from behind the candy counter and placed her hand affectionately on the child's shoulder. Immediately the mother cried out, "Don't do that! Oh! don't do that." The mother turned to Miss Sears and said in a low voice, "You can't tell but what she might bewitch her."[8]

An entirely different recollection is rendered by Norbert Weiner, child mathematical prodigy and eventual founder of the science of cybernetics. From the summer of 1903, when Norbert was eight, his family occupied a farm on Old Mill Road, about a mile from the Shakers. Weiner tells in his autobiography of visiting the Shaker Village with his sister to buy peppermints. Labeling the village a "Protestant Monastery," he wrote, "I remember the venerable Sister Elizabeth, and Sister Anne as well, who retained the worldly coquetry of wearing false hair under her coal scuttle straw bonnet. One or the other would preside at the little shop in their great empty main building. They sold souvenirs and simples, as well as sugared orange peel and enormous disks of sugar—flavored with peppermint and wintergreen. These were ridiculously inexpensive, and were the one sort of sweet which our parents allowed us to eat as far as our appetites might go."[9]

But decline had taken hold in the Shaker communities. In 1901, the Shirley Shakers were forced to tear down the Elijah Wilds house, which had stood since 1771. The timeworn and weather-beaten wooden structure, which had served as sanctuary for the besieged Mother Ann, was considered no longer worth patching.[10]

Membership in the two communities at the turn of the century numbered about two dozen. Marcia Bullard had counted Harvard's membership as "less than forty" in the previous decade.[11] The diaries record numerous defections, especially among the young (who were expected to be virgin as well as celibate). The lure of the world was proving more compelling than in the past. (Many early Shakers had embraced celibacy following several years in the married state and after having raised large families. Might it be that celibacy in such circumstances was as much a relief as a sacrifice?)

In the winter of 1900–1901, Elder John Whiteley's health began to fail seriously. On January 19, the elder recorded that he felt great pain as though struck by a knife in the stomach and lungs. Blank diary pages follow, and Elder John apologizes several days later, stating, "Not able to keep diary for the week follow-ing—But will patch it up a little as I am able for it is a week full of important events—including the death of Queen Victoria." The diary entries trail off after this, and it becomes apparent that Elder John has become totally incapacitated. By spring the diary record stops.

Three years later—on August 16, 1904—the Mount Lebanon ministry came to Shirley and officially released Elder John from the bishopric ministry order and appointed Joseph Holden of Mount Lebanon. Appointed as his associates were Annie L.

Walker and Margaret Eggleson. On February 18, 1905, the local newspaper reported that Whiteley had suffered another shock and there was little hope for his recovery.

The following summer—on August 12, 1905—John Whiteley died at age 86, "after a lingering illness of four years, from the effects of a paralytic shock" in the words of the obituary that appeared in the Ayer newspaper.[12]

Elder Whiteley once told William Dean Howells that he had had a dream while on his voyage to America, a dream so vivid that he wrote down the particulars. When he visited Shirley for the first time he immediately recognized the scene prefigured in his dream. His obituary said of him, "Mr. Whiteley was a man of honest and rugged personality, and by reason of his high principles had earned the respect and esteem of his fellowman. All who knew him testify to the fine qualities he possessed. He loved the Shakers and their principles through the many years of his membership with a devotion that was sincere and unwavering. His lofty character and high ideals will always be a towering monument: to the Shakers, for his fair, frank and open dealings with his fellowmen."[13]

Private funeral services were held in the Church Family of Shakers, with interment in the Shaker Cemetery. Among those who mourned him were his former wife—herself still a faithful Shaker—a son, a daughter, and four grandchildren.

The town of Shirley also felt the loss. As a memorial to its leading Shaker citizen, the town later established Whiteley Park on a tract of land transferred to the town by Elder John in 1896. The gift had raised not a few Shaker eyebrows, especially since news of it first surfaced in the public press and carried with it the stipulation that the park bear Whiteley's name. Eldress Maria Foster wrote in her diary: "We read in the Public Spirit that Elder John has donated a piece of land to Shirley, of the consecrated property, with the proviso, that it shall be called Whiteley Park, quite a retrograde step, from first principles (that we have naught we shall call our own). What next!"[14] Otherwise, reaction to the gift was one of gratitude, and the Whiteley Park Association was established to maintain the property.

After the death of Elder John Whiteley, the leadership of the communities of Harvard and Shirley was predominantly female. Shirley had a mere handful of residents in the final years. The most prominent were eldresses Margaret Eggleson and Josephine Jilson, Laura Beal, Annie Belle Tuttle, Lucy King Mitchell and Mary Ann Whiteley, Elder John's widow. The only male Shaker seems to have been Henry Hollister, a brother of Alonzo Giles Hollister, the Mount Lebanon elder. Hollister spoke of himself as being from Kentucky, according to a Shirley resident who met him. An 1895 document also places him at the short lived Olive Branch Shaker colony at Narcoossee, Osceola County, Florida. Hollister appears to have been assigned to Shirley at the time of John Whiteley's incapacitation.

The only other males at the Shirley village after 1900 were the hired help. A man named Henry Eisner supervised the Shaker milk route. (Eisner's children remembered their father's anger on one occasion, when the hired hands were discovered in a state of drunkenness. The men had been sampling corn liquor that had fermented in the silo. Eisner fired the men on the spot.)

The Shaker who possessed the greatest sensitivity concerning the historical heritage of Shirley was undoubtedly Eldress Josephine Jilson. Josephine was one of five children left fatherless when she was only three years old. Two years later, in 1855, the child and her two sisters were brought to the Shirley Shakers. Her sisters left the community in their teens, but she remained. One acquaintance described Eldress Josephine as a "nice, crisp, businesslike person," and another as a rather stern person who would insist, for instance, that children "sit up straight." She also demonstrated on several occasions a high degree of sentimentality and attachment to her Shaker heritage and principles. It must therefore have pained her deeply to see the razing of the Wilds' house, one of the last visible reminders of the early faith. Eldress Josephine gathered together those items that best reflected the Shaker lifestyle—their inventions, machines, a two-century-old Wilds chair, and other memorabilia—and established a museum of sorts in a woodshed opposite the Church Family office building.

Two events probably triggered the closing of Shirley: one was the loss of John Whiteley, and the other was the appearance of a suitable purchaser for the property; namely, the state of Massachussetts. Whiteley had died in 1905, but a year earlier, when the Mount Lebanon ministry officially relieved him of his title and duties in the bishopric, Elder Joseph Holden of Mount Lebanon had been appointed his successor. Elder Joseph was an expert in real estate matters and would ultimately be involved in directing sales of thousands of acres of Shaker property in Ohio, Florida and Eastern Massachussetts. He seems to have been appointed titular head of the bishopric for the express purpose of disposing of Shirley.

Some Shirley holdings were already gone. The owner of the Samson Cordage Company, James Pike Tolman, had donated the former Shaker land adjacent to Whiteley Park as the site of St. Anthony's French Catholic Church. In 1899, the Brick Tavern, where Howells had stayed, and surrounding land had been sold to Miss Caroline P. Cordner of Boston for the sum of $700. (Miss Cordner was interested in philanthropic work and acquired the property to provide vacation quarters for poor working girls from Boston. Some forty young women from such places as the Franklin Square House were accommodated on a rotating basis for two weeks at a time.) About 1905, the former Shaker infirmary building was moved from the Church Family through the woods about a distance of a mile, and set down adjacent to the Brick Tavern to serve as the caretaker's house.

Following Elder Joseph's arrival, the records show various public auction sales involving miscellaneous land parcels. Those listed as trustees in these transactions were Elder Joseph and Josephine Jilson, Annie Walker and Margaret Eggleson.

The record is less clear concerning an auction of Shaker furnishings and fixtures. Shirley historian Ethel Bolton told of acquiring an 1820 trestle table upon which the coffin of John Whiteley had rested. Mrs. Bolton's husband, Charles K. Bolton, director of the Boston Athenaeum at the time, acquired an old-fashioned carpet loom. Dozens of other Shirley residents purchased Shaker artifacts; many such treasures still grace local homes. Facts concerning this auction have been preserved largely through oral tradition: apparently, the event was not considered newsworthy at the time. A Shirley octogenarian recalled being taken to the auction as a child, just as the auction was ending. Her most vivid memory was of wagons hauling away a quantity of dry sinks.

These auctions were preamble to the closing of the community. About this time the State of Massachussetts was looking for a site to establish an industrial school for boys. The state legislature, in 1907, authorized a feasibility study for a new institution and followed in 1908 with an appropriation to purchase the Shirley Shaker settlement.

Two of the Shirley sisters died early that year and thus were spared the trauma of being dispossessed of their home. Lucy King Mitchell, who had resided at Shirley for fifty-seven years, died at age 73, and Mary Ann Whiteley died two days later on January 9, 1908, at age 89. The widow of Elder John, she was survived by a son in Chicago and a daughter in Leominster.

Prior to the final disposition of the Shirley village, another significant death occurred—that of Olive Hatch. Sister Olive, nicknamed "the great burden bearer," celebrated her one hundredth birthday on September 5, 1908. She had first entered the Shirley Shakers in 1821, coming from Spencer, Massachussetts, in company with her mother, sister, and brother. She lived in Shirley for ten years, moved to Harvard, remained there until 1847, and then was recalled to Shirley to serve as a family eldress. She returned to Harvard in her later years.

In speaking of her life, Sister Olive said, "I have lived nearly all my life among the Shakers, and I have been very happy among the sisters and brothers. I have always been contented and have never longed for any other life. If I had several lives to live and could choose an abiding place on earth, I would spend them all with the Shakers . . . ."[15]

Sister Olive died a month after reaching her centennial year, apparently done in by the excitement of the landmark celebration. The Shakers held an impressive funeral, after which the youngest member of the community was sent after the team to accompany the body to its last resting place in the Harvard Shaker cemetery. A neighboring friend, according to the obituary notice, had "kindly lined the grave with boughs and blossoms," and after the coffin was lowered the assemblage sang a final song of farewell.[16]

The sale of Shaker properties in Shirley and in Lancaster for creation of the Shirley Industrial School was announced on October 3, 1908. The deed was consummated on December 8.[17] The transaction involved 889 acres of land, together with twenty-six buildings, including dwellings, brick office, blacksmith shop, dairy house, workmen's houses, five barns, sisters' houses, tool and corn houses, and miscellaneous buildings, plus livestock. The purchase price was $43,000, held in trust by Elder Joseph of the Central Ministry "to be used as needed."[18]

The few remaining Shakers began to leave. Brother Henry Hollister, who was recovered from rib and collar bone fractures sustained two years before, when he was thrown from a runaway horse carriage, went to the Hancock Shakers. Eldress Margaret Eggleson moved to the Second Family, Mount Lebanon, to be eldress there—no doubt a welcome assignment for her, as she had lived at the Canaan Upper Family before coming to Shirley. Eldress Margaret's place in the ministry was filled by Josephine Jilson, who became family eldress of the Harvard bishopric, and associate in the ministry and trustee with Eldress Annie Walker.[19]

Eldress Josephine, Laura Beal, and Annie Belle Tuttle remained in Shirley until the start of the new year, attending to final details. In the closing days, Eldress Josephine presented approximately one hundred books and a Shaker chair to the Hazen Public Library in Shirley. The titles included fiction, poetry, science and religion, as well as strictly Shaker volumes. The name of Elder John Whiteley appeared on the flyleaf of some of the books. The library also received a set of eggcups which the Whiteleys had brought from England. In expressing gratitude, library trustees stated, "By the removal of the Shaker community, the library has lost most valuable and appreciative patrons."[20]

Eldress Josephine and Sisters Laura and Annie Belle departed Shirley for Harvard the first week of January, 1909. Although it was a time of sadness, the sisters were at least pleased that the new institution would continue the Shaker tradition of providing a good manual education for those who needed it. "It is better," said one of the sisters (probably Eldress Josephine) to a correspondent for the *Boston Transcript*, "for the property to be sold this way than for all of us to die here and have the roofs tumble over us. These are noble people who are going to do this work."[21]

Such brave statements to the contrary, abandonment of Shirley was shattering to those whose lives had been spent there. A Harvard diary entry for January 6, 1909, conveys the sense of loss: "Josephine Jilson, Laura Beal and Annie Belle Tuttle come here from Shirley, all there was left of a once promising society. They have sold the whole place to the state for boys . . . were paid $43,000 . . . poor sisters, they were almost heart broken. Josephine was nearly prostrate, has been sick three weeks, they all had a terrible hard time picking up and straightening out things. I hope they will get at home here."[22]

Administrators of the new state school in Shirley occupied the village soon after the Shakers departed. Workmen were hired to set up dormitories, convert shops, recultivate the fields, and manage the dairy and its twenty-five milking cows. Henry Eisner, who had been in charge of the Shaker milk route for fifteen years, was retained by the state to continue the dairy operation. The school's first superintendent, Herbert F. Taylor, a Dartmouth graduate who had served in several Massachussetts communities as teacher or administrator, instituted a dramatic facelifting of the village. Carpenters, plumbers, electricians and other tradesmen swarmed through the buildings. Heating and ventilating systems were installed, an electric plant was constructed, and new water and sewer systems were introduced. Buildings were equipped with electric bells, telephones and modern plumbing. Narrow treaded stairways were ripped out, and the latest lighting fixtures took the place of candles and small oil lamps. The Shaker office became the new administration building; an infirmary was installed in the former elder's workshop, and two other buildings were converted to dormitories. Fortunately, the meeting house was retained as the chapel, with services to be provided by Catholic and Protestant clergymen; attendance was to be compulsory.

Superintendent Taylor determined to make the institution as nearly self-supporting as possible, and directed that the fields be

planted and the dairy used to supply the school with milk and butter. Three shop buildings were designated for the making of
chairs, tables and other articles. Boys assigned to Shirley would
"put their hands to work"—in the shops, on the farm, in the kitch-
en or in the newly established bakery. Superintendent Taylor
proposed a regime that would stress firm discipline leavened with
kindness, his objective being to rehabilitate the character of his
charges and render them employable as tradesmen, chefs, and
farm helpers upon their departure from Shirley.[23] The first boy
arrived on August 3, 1909; there were ninety-seven commitments
by the end of November.[24]

The addition of the trio of sisters who left Shirley at its closing
brought to about fifteen the number of members in the Harvard
community. Most were of advanced age. A visiting correspondent
wrote that there were only two male members—most likely
Stephen McKnight and Nathaniel Nilant—neither of whom were
able-bodied. The Shaker "community" in the larger sense consisted of workmen and friendly neighbors. Frederick and Dora
Avery lived at the South Family, in the old house formerly used in
the manufacture of applesauce. A family by the name of Lovell
lived across the road. One Charles Dalton was listed as manager of
the village and Bliss Goss as foreman.

Two younger men, Frank Stanton and Frank Hobbs, had
been brought up in the village. Stanton was brought to Harvard
from Boston by Eldress Annie Walker and Maria Foster when he
was eight years old. Eldress Annie took a special liking to young
Frank, and he became very fond of her. The eldress gave Frank a
little card in her own writing, stating that he was born August 30,
1880; Stanton kept this card for the rest of his life. Stanton ven-
tured into the outside world when he was twenty-three, going to
work for the railroad at the Ayer freight yard, but was back with
the Shakers after just two weeks. Though Stanton gradually
attained independence, he always showed affection for his early
home.

Frank Hobbs came to the Shakers after the death of his
parents. His sister, Edith, went to live with an aunt, but Frank,
being frail, was sent to the Shakers in the belief that country air

and the quiet life would do him good. Stanton and Hobbs became like brothers, and Edith Hobbs, who came to visit her brother often, later married Frank Stanton.

The roster of the Harvard membership as the first decade of the twentieth century closed included—besides Brothers Stephen and Nathaniel, Eldresses Annie and Josephine, and Sisters Laura and Annie Belle—Louisa E. Green and her daughter, Ellen, Maria Wood, Myra McLean, Hattie Whitney, and Lottie Tremper. A few other names flit in and out of the journals—notably Mary Ashley and Florence Foye—as relocations back and forth between Mount Lebanon and Harvard or extended stays with relatives confuse the record.

Because their numbers were so few, the Shakers rented out some of their buildings, but continued to use several themselves. The Square House was rented to a succession of people; eventually it was used by Eldress Josephine as a museum for her curios. The small house next to the Square House was known as the tailor shop; across from that was Brother Stephen's shop for mending harnesses and making general repairs. Dora Avery attended worship services in the bellhouse and joined with the Shakers in singing "Zion, Thou Still Art Strong," led by Ellen Green, a family eldress.

Mrs. Avery described life in the Harvard village as she observed it during those years.[25] The first eldress, she said, had charge of the clothing and supplies; the second was in charge of the kitchen supplies and household goods. In the long dining room were tables set in squares, four settings to each square. Places at the table were reserved for head eldresses, head sisters, head brothers, foot sisters, and so on. After marching to table in silence, the Shakers knelt in wordless prayer, seated themselves, and ate in silence, speaking—if necessary—only in a whisper. Over the table, hanging on chains from the ceiling, were old-fashioned casters holding vinegar, salt, and pepper. With this feature and with the family style servings for four, there was no need for asking to pass the food and condiments. The dining room was cared for by the dining room sister, who also washed dishes, made tea and coffee, set the table and served the bread and butter. Another sister, perhaps with a helper, presided over the bakery room. The sisters were on monthly rotation in these and other tasks. (Eldress Annie was especially famed for her delicious baked beans while Sister Lottie and Sister Hattie were noted for their apple and mince pies respectively.)

Sister Louisa Green, who had been eldress at the South Family before its closing, relinquished her title when she came to live at the Church Family. She and Sister Maria Woods and—most likely—Louisa's daughter, Eldress Ellen, occupied the First House. Louisa was expert at tailoring and did the mending for the brothers.

Louisa's son, Newcomb, and his wife, Gertrude, remained in the vicinity of the Shaker village following their marriage. Their union was a happy and prolific one, but it ended prematurely with the death of Gertrude at twenty-eight, following the birth of her fourth child. A Shaker journal recorded the sad event in an entry for August 30, 1896—". . . Myra [McLean] went to Newcomb's to help there, on Saturday afternoon Gerty or Gertrude Green passed over the dark river to her eternal home, about midnight. Newcomb is now left with four small children. I pity him."[26] Newcomb kept the three older children, but placed the infant for adoption. He later married Ella Patten, a native of Reading, Massachussetts, and had two more children. He continued to visit the Shakers with his family, which eventually included a grandchild.

Opposite the First House where Louisa lived was the Shaker office, containing the store where peppermints, baskets, rugs and other articles were for sale. The office was also the residence for Eldress Annie and a number of other sisters. The parlor had black walnut furniture padded with hair cloth—certainly a departure from the classic era of Shaker furnishings. Pictures of departed Shakers hung on the walls about the room. It was in the office building that visitors from among the world's people—guests or persons on business—were received.

Among these guests was Clara Endicott Sears, who began summering in Harvard in 1910 and who was in the process of establishing a museum at Fruitlands to commemorate the Alcott utopian experiment. Miss Sears was a wealthy Bostonian, a descendant of two colonial governors, Endicott and Winthrop, and drawn to American history. (Her writings include New England histories, romantic novels in the style of Hawthorne, and the hymn "Unfurling of the Flag.") Miss Sears's main Shaker contact appears to have been Eldress Josephine, but she most likely met others who died before the middle of the decade. (Eldress Annie died in 1912 at age 64. Three died in 1914—Brother Stephen, 84; Maria Wood, 95; and Louisa Green, 90. Ellen Green died the year after her mother, in March 1915, at age 71.)

Miss Sears was the first to dramatize the vanishing Shaker legacy. Her book, *Gleanings From Old Shaker Journals*, published in 1916, salvaged much of what otherwise might have been lost. Eldress Josephine was pleased with Miss Sears's book; in later years she ordered copies from Miss Sears to give as Christmas presents.

The Shakers visited Fruitlands when the first museum opened in the old Alcott farmhouse. Responding to Miss Sears's invitation and using a carriage furnished by her, twelve of the Shakers inspected the Prospect Hill property on June 30, 1914, and posed for photographs.

Miss Elvira Scorgie, a student of Harvard town history, and her older sister, Anna, visited the Shakers about 1915. Anna wanted to learn how to operate a spinning wheel for her role in a Colonial-era play sponsored by the Harvard Women's Club. Where better to observe the art of spinning than at the Shakers! The ladies were cordially received by Eldress Josephine and the other sisters, who then proceeded to give a willing demonstration of the art of spinning. The Scorgies thought them quite happy.

On June 29, 1917, the *Clinton Item* reported in its pages a rumor that Fiske Warren was considering purchasing the Shaker holdings: "The village includes about 600 acres of land and in the last valuation published is listed as taxed for $12,125 personal and $44,210 [real]. . . . At present, there are 12 Shakers still living in the village but they intend moving to the Rural Home in the near future." The newspaper conjecture turned out to be partly true, but was premature by about a year.

The decision finally came to disband the Harvard community

and to sell the land and buildings. The deed to the property, which was purchased by Fiske Warren for $60,000, was signed on April 15, 1918, by the four members of the Central Ministry: Joseph Holden, Walter Shepherd, Sarah Burger and M. Catherine Allen.[27] The decision to close Harvard, though not unexpected, was traumatic for those affected, especially the heritage-minded Eldress Josephine, who had to abandon her Shirley home a decade earlier. Once again furniture and other possessions were put up for sale. The Scorgie sisters, who had visited the community on a happy mission three years earlier, paid a last call. This time they found the sisters in tears. Eldress Josephine appeared so distressed as she showed them articles for sale that the Scorgies cut their visit short, purchased two chairs, and left.

Eldress Josephine took steps to insure that cherished objects would be preserved for posterity. Miss Sears had requested and been promised the rocking chair used by Mother Ann at the Square House. The chair had been appropriated for the more or less exclusive use of Brother Nathaniel, who claimed that it was so made that it would fit anybody comfortably. Miss Sears recognized that the Windsor-style rocker was of priceless historical interest, but she was denied possession when she first asked for it. "Nay, not yet," Eldress Josephine replied, "for Brother Nathaniel would not be able to live without his chair. He rests himself continually in it." Brother Nathaniel confirmed this, stating, "Oh! yea, I must keep the chair until I go." As the village was breaking up, then, the chair was given to Miss Sears.[28]

Eldress Josephine also presented Miss Sears with artifacts from Holy Hill—an old hinge, hasp, and key. "Now we go," she said tearfully to Miss Sears, "and give thee the key of the Holy Hill."[29]

Arrangements were made to relocate the last Shakers to Mount Lebanon or to provide for those who wished to remain in the Harvard area. The aged Brother Nathaniel was "well situated" in a home paid for monthly. Hattie Whitney elected to "go outside" to live with friends. She was given $1,000 and all the furniture and bedding she desired. Myra McLean, a Civil War widow who "had access" to an unspecified pension of $300 annually, requested and received a monthly allotment of $12.50. A semi-invalid referred to in the record only as "Jane _____ was to receive "according to self stated needs." Bessie Bailey, "not a member," was "sufficiently helped"—according to Shaker records.[30]

Frank Stanton and Edith Hobbs were among those who helped the Shakers move.[31] Stanton supervised the transfer of the horses still owned by the Shakers, riding in the train boxcar with them so they would be less frightened. Five truckloads of furniture and personal belongings also had to be moved.

When the time came for the sisters to leave Harvard, Eldress Josephine, Sister Laura Beal, Sister Annie Belle Tuttle, Sister Sadie Maynard and Sister Lottie Tremper bade a loving farewell to the many dear friends who had come to see them off.[32]

Upon reaching Mount Lebanon, Eldress Josephine and Sisters Laura, Annie Belle and Sadie were assigned to the North Family. Sister Lottie moved to the Church Family and on her behalf the sum of $1,000 was paid by Eldress Josephine to Emma J. Neale of the Church Family.[33]

For the first time in 136 years the Shaker Holy Land was bereft of members; all that remained were buildings, fields, woodland, and graves.

10. The Ancient Landmarks

Fiske WARREN, who purchased the Harvard Shaker holdings, was a social experimenter.[1] Warren first entertained a scheme to utilize several hundred acres of Shaker land as a farm to be worked by returning veterans of World War I.[2] This plan fizzled, however, because of lack of interest on the part of veterans, and the soldier colony that he envisioned on land formerly tilled by Shaker pacifists never materialized.

Warren was a leading exponent of the single-tax theory popularized by Henry George, whose book *Progress and Poverty*, published in 1879, condemned private property ownership as the curse of civilization. George contended that economic progress was inhibited by a growing scarcity of land, and that idle land-owners were harvesting a disproportionate return at the expense of such productive elements as labor and capital; he proposed a tax on land values only, eliminating all other taxes. Improvements made upon land would reduce, rather than raise, taxes. Such an economic panacea captured the fancy of a public that had just endured the depression of 1873–78. His book sold millions of copies, and George was a significant political force until his death in 1897.

154

George's theories, directed at curing poverty and inequality, had humanitarian and religious appeal. The Shakers were responsive to his views. Elder Frederick Evans, who frequently advocated land limitation, corresponded with him. Daniel Fraser, then at Mount Lebanon following his stint in the ministry at Shirley, wrote a letter of Shaker support when George was a candidate for mayor of New York in 1886; the letter appeared in the New York *Tribune* of December 23. (George narrowly lost to the Democratic candidate, Abram Hewitt, but ran substantially ahead of the Republican candidate, Theodore Roosevelt.)

In attempting to apply George's formula, Warren began to acquire property in Harvard. He launched Tahanto, his single-tax community, with the lease of two lots of land in 1909. The acquisition of the Shaker lands was a logical expansion, seemingly tailormade for his grand design. Handicapped in having to superimpose the single tax over the existing tax structure, he nevertheless hoped to demonstrate the validity of the theory. Tahanto trustees paid town taxes and certain state and federal taxes from the economic rent on 99-year leases and refunded the money to the leaseholders.

The scheme relied heavily on Warren's personal wealth; upon his death in 1938, the noble dream ended. Warren's heirs chose not to pursue the experiment, and Tahanto holdings, including properties in Shaker Village, were sold. The buildings became privately owned residences.

The one exception was the small original Church Family office building. This, the fourth structure erected by the Harvard Shakers (in 1795) and last used as the men's shop, was purchased from Warren by Miss Sears to house a Shaker museum. It was relocated to the Fruitlands hillside near the Alcott farmhouse. (Miss Sears experienced some delay in acquiring the property; Warren was apparently obliged to clear title to his holdings. One account mentions "some procedures at law," and there are hints that, following the departure of the Shakers, certain parties attempted to make claims on land given by ancestors.) When the building was moved, Miss Sears was particular that the contractor replace every board, clapboard and timber in exactly its original position. One of the two mounting platforms at the South Family[3]

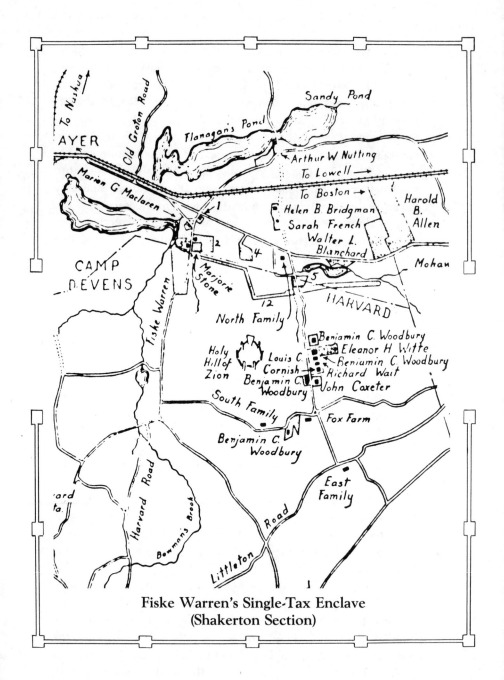

Fiske Warren's Single-Tax Enclave
(Shakerton Section)

156

was also relocated to the museum site. Stone posts and flagstones from the village were used to landscape and enclose the lawn about the house. Stone steps at the South Family, believed to have been trod by Mother Ann, were also transferred. The building opened to the public on June 4, 1921, the first Shaker museum in the country.[4]

Miss Sears was encouraged in her preservation efforts by Eldress Josephine and by Central Ministry Eldress M. Catherine Allen, both of whom corresponded with Miss Sears and sent box-loads of articles. Eldress Josephine frequently sent regards from "the Harvard Club"—meaning herself and others relocated to Mount Lebanon: Sisters Laura, Annie Belle, and Sadie.

The fifth member of the group, Lottie Tremper, left the Shakers and got married. Though it was unexpected, the circumstances of her marriage, at age 60, are quite understandable. Believers who were uprooted from Shaker villages often had difficulty adjusting to new surroundings. Sister Lottie (short for Charlotte) missed her former ramblings around Harvard and was concerned about her security in old age. Her life had been a series of dislocations. Born an only child in the town of Sand Lake, Rensselaer County, New York, in 1860, she was taken to the Shakers in Canaan, where her aunt, Louisa Green, was second eldress. She lived there until she was eighteen. Among her friends was her second cousin, who lived in nearby Lebanon Springs.

Sister Lottie was transferred to the Harvard South Family in 1878. She was joined by her aunt and others from Canaan when that community was broken up in 1884. Her aunt Louisa became eldress of the family.

Within a few months of coming to New Lebanon, after the Harvard community closed, Lottie looked up her childhood friend, whom she had not seen for forty years. She agreed to become his third wife the following September; her married name was Gillette. The couple lived in Providence, Rhode Island until 1926 and then moved to Ayer, making their home with Mrs. Ella Green, widow of Newcomb Green, Eldress Louisa's son.[5] Lottie worked as a housekeeper in 1928 with the Fred Sanderson family of Shirley, whose house was in the neighborhood of the former Shirley Shakers; she often spoke of her life among the Shakers.

Lottie Tremper Gillette died of pneumonia on November 30, 1929, one month short of her seventieth birthday. She was laid to rest in the Shaker Cemetery in Harvard; the last burial in the cemetery.[6]

Also buried in the Harvard Shaker Cemetery in the years following the community's closing were Nathaniel Nilant, who died in 1920, and Myra McLean, who died in 1923. Six months before her death, Sister Myra paid a call at Fruitlands to see the Shaker Museum and to visit with Miss Sears. She saw Mother Ann's chair and other artifacts on display, including the funeral plank on which Shaker dead were measured for a coffin. The aged sister lamented the loss of the happy life she had known. "And to think," she said, "that I shall never lie upon that plank. Eldress Louisa lay upon it. Eldress Ellen Green and Olive Hatch and all the dear eldresses and sisters, but I am denied it. But I shall sleep in the Shaker burying ground with them and we shall all be together."[7]

In the Shaker Museum, Miss Sears gathered photographs of the leading elders and eldresses, together with diaries, manuscripts, and old Shaker imprints. She purchased the bell from the East Family—dated 1833 and initialed G.H.H. It has been rung during the tourist season ever since to signal the daily closing of the Fruitlands Museums.[8] A gravestone from the Shirley community—given by Shirley Industrial School—was installed on the back lawn of the museum, but it was later removed. The stone, still in possession of the museum, is lettered "L. Hayward, dec'd March 1822 Age 75."[9] Miss Sears invited Eldress Josephine and Eldress M. Catherine Allen of the ministry to attend the opening of the museum, but neither was able to accept. Eldress Catherine died in June 1922 without ever seeing the museum, but Eldress Josephine, who visited Harvard every summer until 1925—calling on Mrs. Avery and other friends and also arranging for the upkeep of the Shaker Cemetery—did tour the museum and was delighted with it.

Eldress Josephine was joined at Mount Lebanon by a sister, Henrietta Ophelia Jilson, in the summer of 1924. Henrietta had left the Shirley Shakers in 1866 as a teenager, had married, and had raised a son. Henrietta died in the fall and was brought to Taunton, Massachusetts, for burial.[10] The following year, on November 16, 1925, at the age of 75, Josephine Jilson died, following a ten-day hospitalization at the House of Mercy in Pittsfield. Ministry Elder Walter Shepherd arranged to have the body removed to Shirley and presided at the funeral service and burial at the Shaker Cemetery there. Eldress Josephine's was the last interment at the former Shirley Shaker Village, a testimonial to her abiding love for the community where she had spent fifty-three years. Two years after her death, the individual gravestones were removed, and a single monument was erected to honor all who slept there. It bears the inscription: "Erected by the United Society of Shakers to Honor the Memory of Members Interred in this Lot 1792–1925."[11]

During the early 1930s, the first interest was stirring in Harvard to reclaim the Shaker heritage. Dr. Benjamin C. Woodbury, who occupied one of the Church Family buildings, the Second House, wrote verses commemorating the shops, dwellings, cemetery and other holy places in the village. It was his hope that the Shaker atmosphere of the village could be saved and that Shaker handiwork and furniture which had been scattered be brought back. Thanks to his foresight and to private owners like him, the character of the village kept its Shaker charm. Formal preservation efforts were to take shape in the 1960s.

Some structures, however, were altered or destroyed. The South Family office building burned in the mid-1920s. The large South Family dwelling survived, but its exterior appearance belied its use for several years as the Avery chicken house. Before that, it had served as a tuberculosis contact house, a place where children from the Boston area who had contact with TB but did not have the disease could spend a healthful summer; Mrs. Avery had as many as sixty girls living at the dwelling in the late 1920s and early 1930s. The South Family barn survived until 1975, when it collapsed.

At the Church Family, some buildings either disintegrated or burned. Both the Square House and meeting house survived as residences, the meeting house radically partitioned. The Great

Barn, rebuilt after the 1894 fire, burned again in 1937. The schoolhouse, originally located north of the Square House, was relocated to a site opposite the cemetery, but later, badly deteriorated, was swept by fire.

The Harvard Historical Society sponsored occasional pilgrimages through the village. One such tour of landmarks and buildings[12] in the summer of 1933 also served as a reunion of sorts for persons formerly associated with the community. About sixty persons took part, among them Frank and Edith Stanton, Laura Beal, Mary Ashley, and Arthur West. The group visited the monument where Father James Whittaker and William Lee had been whipped. At the South Family, Mrs. Avery sounded the bell which had once summoned believers to work and worship. Stopping by the old cemetery, they noted the advanced ages on the grave markers. The group continued their pilgrimage past buildings of the Church Family, and some even climbed the former Holy Hill.

On September 21, 1938, New England was battered by a mighty hurricane. Damage in central Massachusetts towns was extensive. Many of the Norway spruces set out by the Shakers were toppled; one of them damaged the roof of the Square House in falling. The old cart shed in Harvard blew over and collapsed on a car stored inside.[13] (The cart shed had been raised on April 15, 1845. The Shaker journal for that day concluded, "So here is recorded when the form of this building was first exhibited, and what will be its fate, whether burn down, blow down, be pulled down, or rot down, time only will prove."[14]) At the South Family, a large tree barely missed striking the Avery homestead.

The Rural Home was torn down in 1939. It had been a hotel, a health retreat, and finally a residence, and also stood vacant for several years. Its last use was as a refuge for an Ayer family whose house had been destroyed in the hurricane.[15] No trace of the Rural Home remains, and only one building of the Harvard North Family of which the Rural Home was a part continues in existence.

The Shaker cemetery in Harvard, in contrast to the Rural Home, has remained relatively undisturbed. Secluded off South Shaker road between the South Family and the Church Family, it is a peaceful and picturesque spot surrounded by gnarled old trees and a border of lilies of the valley. There are ten rows of graves, averaging thirty to a row. A total of 312 Shakers are buried there; the first interment was that of Susannah Willard, who died October 3, 1792.[16] The bodies of six other sisters buried on a nearby knoll in the previous decade were later exhumed and deposited in one coffin for reinterment. An early document also states that "it will be perceived on reading the following list of interment that there are graves in the midst of some of the rows, and some near the head of others of a far more recent date than those below them. With a few exceptions, this has come in consequence of deep snows in our Northern climate in winter seasons, and those employed as grave diggers not being able to ascertain the grave immediately below."[17]

Grave monuments include markers made of cast iron with raised lettering, giving the names and dates of birth and death; small granite stones were also used. Beginning in 1921, the cemetery was cared for by members of the Harvard Woman's Club; Eldress Josephine contributed $100 to assist the club in the cemetery's upkeep. In 1941, the town of Harvard agreed to accept the cemetery as a gift, the land to be used exclusively as a Shaker cemetery. The sum of $100, with interest, was also accepted and was placed in trust.[18] Some of the grave markers have been damaged over the years, there have been acts of vandalism, and the lettering on some of the stones has grown indistinct. Generally, however, townspeople have treated the cemetery with reverence.

The Shirley Shaker cemetery, meanwhile, was maintained by work crews from Shirley Industrial School. Some uncertainty exists as to what became of the original gravestones replaced by the single monument in 1927. According to one account, at least some of the stones were used in the base of the new monument. Some stones may have been placed about the buildings to serve as rain deflectors under the downspouts, as was done at Canterbury. However, examination with a cemetery probing rod indicates that stones are buried under the topsoil.

Efforts to preserve the old Shirley buildings have been unspectacular, particularly as new buildings were erected on the school grounds and older structures fell into disuse. Several buildings were destroyed by fire. The old icehouse with its sawdust-insulated walls was blown down in the 1938 hurricane.

Shirley Industrial School accommodated between two and three hundred boys at capacity before its closing in 1971. The boys were split into groups and placed under the supervision of cottage masters. One of these, a Scotch immigrant named Archie Patterson, came to the school to teach masonry in 1934. One day Patterson came upon a massive stone object overgrown with bushes near the icehouse. On closer inspection, the object turned out to be the great watering trough that Howells had mentioned in his writings more than a half century earlier. Patterson relocated the old horse trough to a spot under one of the old elm trees at the site of the former Wilds house and planted flowers in the hollowed bowl. Patterson was most impressed with an iron staple which the Shakers had embedded in the horse trough to keep a crack in the stone from opening.

One of the more unusual adaptations of the buildings at Shirley was the use of the North Family office building as a State Police barracks. Troopers were regularly called upon to pursue boys who fled the school, but the site was otherwise too isolated. The Shirley barracks was abandoned in 1957 when a new barracks opened beside Route 2 in Leominster.

The old Shirley meeting house, fortunately, remained in a good state of preservation. First used as a chapel by the state, it later became a social center. The Woman's Club of the school met there; it was used for faculty meetings and for staging dinners after athletic events. An interesting alteration was the removal of two sections of board in which had been carved heart-shaped apertures. These were thought to have been used for surveillance of activities in the worship hall from ministry quarters on the second floor. The third floor also had sleeping chambers which were available to visiting ministries.

In 1962, a group restoring Hancock Shaker Village in western Massachusetts obtained permission from the state to have the Shirley meeting house relocated to Hancock. The former Hancock meeting house had been dismantled in 1938. The Shirley building was purchased from the state for one dollar, and the money to finance the relocation was provided by Mrs. Maud Moon Weyerhaeuser Sanborn, whose first husband was part of the family that created the West Coast lumber empire. A Swampscott firm of moving specialists removed and numbered all the clapboards, cut the building in nine sections, and transported the sections atop flatbed trucks on a 122-mile, police-escorted trip across the state to its new location high in the Berkshires. When reassembled, the building looked as it did in Shirley. The great stone watering trough was moved to Hancock at the same time, along with three trestle tables.

The meeting house was rededicated at ceremonies on May 30, 1963, before the opening of Hancock's third season as a Shaker restoration. A panel of speakers reviewed the history of the Shakers, telling about the work of master builder Moses Johnson and about Mother Ann Lee. Shaker songs were sung—"Come life, Shaker life! Come life eternal; shake, shake out of me all that is carnal," was one refrain. The group attending the dedication were impressed by the liveliness of the Shaker tunes and such straightforward lyrics as "Mother's wine is working . . . I'll be reeling, turning, twisting . . . Shake out all the starch and stiff'ning."[19]

When Shirley gave up its meeting house, it lost the centerpiece of what remained of the Shaker village, but the move saved the building from scheduled demolition by the state. Use of the remaining dozen or so Shaker buildings declined as the number of boys at Shirley Industrial School decreased and as newer state-constructed buildings proved more than adequate to accommodate the population. Shirley Industrial School was phased out of existence in 1971. A private drug rehabilitation program called Spectrum House occupied three of the cottages for a time. Then the facility was converted to a pre-release center for prisoners preparing for parole, and a training school for prison guards was subsequently established.

In 1975, the former Shirley Shaker Village was included in the National Register of Historic Places, an effort spearheaded by a historically minded Shirley resident, artist and writer Sandy Farnsworth. There was no accompanying strategy, however, for restoring the largely unoccupied and deteriorating Shaker buildings. (Unfortunately from a preservation point of view, the most dramatic change to follow the historic designation was the erection in 1978 of a new water tower at the former Shirley Holy Hill. This replaced an outmoded water tower on a hill behind the North Family barn. All trace of the Shaker worship ground has been obliterated by construction of the water tower. Only photographs of the Shirley Fountain Stone remain; the tablet itself disappeared long ago.)

The Brick Tavern remains in use as a dwelling just beyond the borders of Shirley. During the Great Depression, the Federal Writers' Project in its Massachusetts volume of the American Guide Series acknowledged the historical associations of the stagecoach house and that of the adjacent "hospital," which it said had a room "with a closet said to have been used by the Shakers for disciplinary purposes. Latched on the outside, the door to the closet contains a heart-shaped aperture through which recalcitrant members were watched or fed."[20] Actually, the purpose of the aperture is unclear and could have been decorative, symbolic, or functional. If the latter, the opening may have been for ventilation or for surveillance of the sickly or quarantined.

The old Shaker Mills, built in the middle of the nineteenth century for manufacture of bedsheets and cotton cloth, has undergone numerous name changes but is still in active business use, manufacturing maritime rope as large as three feet thick.

Modern Shirley has other reminders of its Shaker inheritance, including the names of many of its streets and roads. Gone, however, are the roads that once provided direct access to the Still River section of Harvard and its train stop; these now terminate at the boundaries of Fort Devens.

The world has changed drastically since the last Shakers left their Holy Land; the time of their departure now seems remote. But some of the last Shakers and those who shared their lives in the Harvard and Shirley villages survived to witness many of the climactic events of this century. The daughter of Elder John and Mary Whiteley—Mrs. Sarah E. Burns—lived to age 95 and died at her home in Leominster in 1938. Sisters Annie Belle Tuttle and Sadie Maynard survived to midcentury. A person who visited

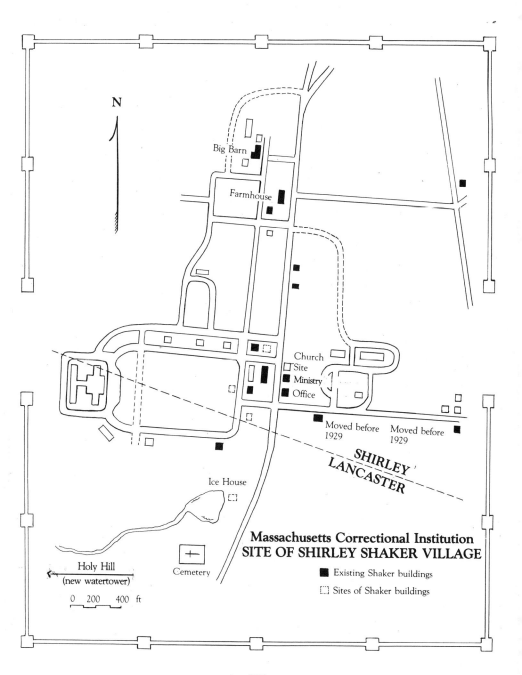

N

Big Barn

Farmhouse

Church
Site
Ministry
Office

Moved before
1929

Moved before
1929

SHIRLEY
LANCASTER

Ice House

Holy Hill
(new watertower)

Cemetery

0   200   400 ft

Massachusetts Correctional Institution
SITE OF SHIRLEY SHAKER VILLAGE

■ Existing Shaker buildings
□ Sites of Shaker buildings

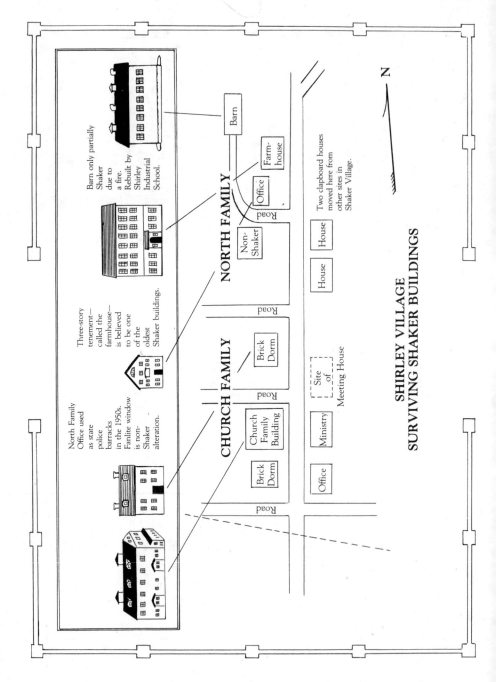

SHIRLEY VILLAGE
SURVIVING SHAKER BUILDINGS

Barn only partially due to a fire. Rebuilt by Shirley Industrial School.

Three-story tenement—called the farmhouse—is believed to be one of the oldest Shaker buildings.

North Family Office used as state police barracks in the 1950s. Fanlite window is non-Shaker alteration.

Two clapboard houses moved here from other sites in Shaker Village.

NORTH FAMILY

CHURCH FAMILY

Barn

Farm-house

Office

Non-Shaker

Road

House

House

House

Road

Brick Dorm

Site of Meeting House

Ministry

Road

Church Family Building

Brick Dorm

Office

Road

N

them at Mount Lebanon remembers them as sad and lonely, qualities often found in those who had been transferred from one community to another. Sister Annie Belle, who had a reputation for being considerate of visiting children—taking them to the kitchen for cookies and the like—maintained a collection of Shaker memorabilia in a basement of the North Family, a miniature museum of Shaker furniture, small items, and scraps of poetry composed by various sisters. She came alive when requested to show the collection; it had clearly become a shrine to her. Sister Sadie tagged along holding the hand of the visitor.

Sister Annie Belle died at Pittsfield's House of Mercy in 1945, at age 77, and was buried at Mount Lebanon. Sister Sadie—often referred to as "Little Sadie" because of her petite stature—went to Hancock to live when Mount Lebanon closed in the mid-1940s. She died at the Hancock colony in 1953, and was buried there.

Sister Laura Beal, another member of the group that Eldress Josephine once styled "the Harvard Club," became disenchanted at Mount Lebanon and left there five years after arriving from Harvard. She returned to the Harvard area in 1923 and, for the last seventeen years of her life, took up residence with a family in Ayer. She was a member of the town's Federated Church, a union of Methodist, Baptist, and Congregational parishioners. She died in 1946, at age 80, and was buried in the town's Woodlawn Cemetery.[21]

The passage of time has stilled at last all living echoes from the Shaker Holy Land. Even the landscape has changed to veil the physical traces of the Shaker villages. The old byways that once connected village and town have been much obliterated. A new superhighway, Route 2, has further transformed area geography with a half dozen bridges and overpasses between Harvard and Lancaster. Opened in 1953, this highway necessitated the razing of the former Harvard East Family buildings, which had badly deteriorated after sale by the Shakers in 1890.

In 1963, an organization called Shakerton Foundation and headed by architect Bayard Underwood was incorporated to record and preserve the remaining Shaker buildings in Harvard.

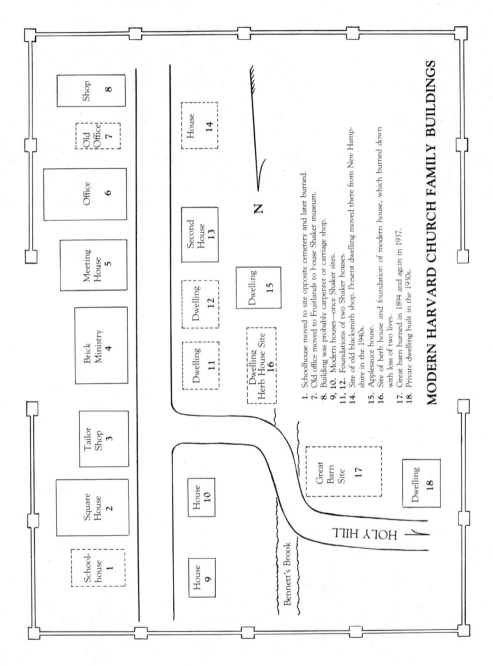

Building	Description
1.	Schoolhouse moved to site opposite cemetery and later burned.
7.	Old office moved to Fruitlands to house Shaker museum.
8.	Building was probably carpenter or carriage shop.
9, 10.	Modern houses—once Shaker sites.
11, 12.	Foundations of two Shaker houses.
14.	Site of old blacksmith shop. Present dwelling moved there from New Hampshire in the 1940s.
15.	Applesauce house.
16.	Site of herb house and foundation of modern house, which burned down with loss of two lives.
17.	Great barn burned in 1894 and again in 1937.
18.	Private dwelling built in the 1930s.

School-house 1 · Square House 2 · Tailor Shop 3 · Brick Ministry 4 · Meeting House 5 · Office 6 · Old Office 7 · Shop 8

House 9 · House 10 · Dwelling 11 · Dwelling 12 · Second House 13 · House 14 · Dwelling 15 · Dwelling Herb House Site 16 · Great Barn Site 17 · Dwelling 18

Bennett's Brook

HOLY HILL

N

MODERN HARVARD CHURCH FAMILY BUILDINGS

Underwood's measured drawings, along with National Park Service photographs of Shaker buildings, have been filed with the Library of Congress as part of the Historic American Buildings series.

In 1972, Harvard citizens voted to make the Church Family and Holy Hill sections of the Shaker village a historic district, insuring that future building alterations be subject to approval by a Historic District Commission. Two years later, the district was expanded to include the South Family. A major investment in restoring Holy Hill followed. The Harvard Conservation Commission, aided by state and federal funding, purchased 103 acres of land in the area of Holy Hill. The former "dancing ground" was cleared, a replica of the old Shaker fence was built, and historic markers were erected. The surrounding area, which was developing residentially, was laced with a network of hiking, horse, and cross-country ski trails. Contractors also cleared land for a playing field. Including the value of some parcels of donated land, the project cost $242,420.

On May 21, 1976, the Holy Hill project was dedicated. Eldresses Bertha Lindsay and Gertrude Soule of the Canterbury, New Hampshire Shakers joined with local, state, and federal dignitaries at the formal ceremonies. Eldress Gertrude offered her gratitude in behalf of the Shakers to officials present, extending her arms in the Shaker gesture of "giving love" and instructing her hearers in the reciprocal gesture of "gathering love." A local speaker instrumental in promoting the project, Erhart Muller of the village, stated, "This land was sacred to the Shakers, and it is sacred to us." The Shaker eldresses led the assemblage in singing "Simple Gifts."[22]

In July 1977, a group from Sabbathday Lake Community visited Harvard and toured the village. The group, led by Sister Mildred Barker and by Theodore Johnson, director of Sabbathday Lake's museum, comprised students from the University of Maine who were enrolled in a Shaker seminar conducted by Johnson. Village residents assisted as guides. When the group visited the Square House, Sister Mildred paused in silent prayer in the upstairs bedroom where, tradition holds, Mother Ann Lee slept.

Those present, irrespective of their own religious beliefs, seemed to sense that past and present merged on that occasion. The stillness became haunted by the imagined din of ghostly mob members assembling angrily on the lawn below.

Sisters at Harvard, from left, Ellen Green, Eliza Babbitt, Marsha Bullard, Margaret Eggleson, and Annie Walker. (Courtesy of Elmer R. Pearson)

One of the last group photographs of the Harvard Shakers. (Courtesy of Fruitlands Museums)

The huge Harvard Church Family office building was used to accommodate guests. Business with the "world's people" was conducted here, and it was here that the sisters sold peppermints and other fancy goods. (Courtesy of the Library of Congress)

Harvard grouping taken about 1905 shows Shakers and visitors. Children in the foreground and two younger women at the right are attired in the costume of the day and are not Shakers. (Courtesy of the Harvard Historical Society)

Brick Tavern, at left, looking much as it did when Howells stayed there, and the Shaker infirmary building, which was moved to this site about a mile through the woods about the time Shirley was closing.

Single monument and plaque replaced individual gravestones at Shirley. Plaque reads, "Erected by the United Society of Shakers to honor the memory of the members interred in this lot, 1792-1925." (Photographs by the author)

Shirley North Family barn, shown above, burned after being struck by lightning in 1914. An existing barn on the site is only partly Shaker, most of it having been built by Shirley Industrial School. (Courtesy of Paul Dickhaut)

Buildings in the Shirley North Family. Brick structure is the former office building, which was renovated to include a fanlight front top window and was used as a State Police Barracks in the 1950s. Other buildings no longer exist. (Courtesy of Paul Dickhaut)

(Courtesy of Fruitlands Museums)

Former Harvard sisters in their later years. At top, Sadie Maynard and Annie Belle Tuttle. At right, Laura Beal, who left the New Lebanon community in 1923 and spent the rest of her life as a resident of Ayer, Massachusetts. (Courtesy of Katherine Dufresne)

Museum founder Clara Endicott Sears (Photograph by Bachrach, courtesy of Fruitlands Museums)

Mounting platform, or horseblock (lower right), *which once stood in front of the Harvard South Family dwelling, is now at a private residence in Groton. The mounting platform at Fruitlands Museums was formerly at the office building of the South Family. (Photograph by the author)*

Ann Lee's chair (lower left), *a Windsor chair converted to a rocker. (Courtesy of Fruitlands Museums)*

Eldress Bertha Lindsay, left, Eldress Gertrude Soule, and Erhart Muller have tea following dedication of Harvard Holy Hill Project in 1976. (Photograph by Edward Dillard)

A section of the Shirley Meeting House is moved to Hancock aboard a flatbed truck. (Courtesy of Hancock Shaker Museum)

Eldresses Emma King and Gertrude Soule in Hancock at the former Shirley Meeting House. (Courtesy of Hancock Shaker Museum)

11. Now and Tomorrow

THE MAIN DRAMA of the Shaker story has concluded, though a handful of adherents espouse the faith in a final, uncertain epilogue.

Whatever remains to be enacted in the Shaker saga may be found at the two villages of Canterbury, New Hampshire and Sabbathday Lake, Maine. Picturesquely situated on upland rural settings, the villages in winter are menaced by blizzard and wind, but during the summer the airy, sun-drenched complexes are invaded by scores of tourists. Youthful tour guides and maintenance staff abound at this time, but afterwards the villages revert to relative isolation. Only the resident sisters—with perhaps one or two hired hands—remain.

Apart from lingering tourist interest, is Shakerism dead? Some think so, others predict a renaissance. Most commentators, it must be said, have already dug the Shaker grave on the social landscape, indifferent to whatever vital signs remain. Conventional wisdom has been that time will soon extinguish whatever remains of the Shaker institution. Meanwhile, historians analyze the Shaker decline following its peak influence more than a century ago.

It is too simplistic to conclude that celibacy caused the downfall of the Shakers. True, the Shakers, by remaining celibate, forfeited the usual source of recruits available to other groups, but their own annihilation was by no means thus ordained. On the contrary, while non-celibate communal groups withered, Shakerism expanded through conversions over several generations.

Those Shaker historians inclined to accept the validity of divine inspiration are comfortable with the theory that the Shaker inspiration had run out, or, in Shaker parlance, that the gift had come to the end of its season.

The most pragmatic theory is that Shakerism fell victim to economic changes: mass production, conversion to steam power, the rise of the railroads, and so on. Though the Shakers were not disdainful of technological advances, they were unable to maintain the quality of handcrafted articles while using machines, and were reluctant to turn out inferior merchandise. Their products became uncompetitively priced, and they even began increasingly to purchase outside goods. Each such purchase surrendered a measure of self-sufficiency.

The second half of the nineteenth century saw a general decline in the popularity of communalism; one utopian society after another closed. At the same time, the opening of the West and a shift from rural life to urban centers siphoned off the young and adventurous. The ravages of the Civil War hurt Shaker communities, especially those in the South. Afterwards, religious revivals, which had promoted membership in the Shakers, occurred less frequently. In the financial panic of 1873, the Shaker economy was further hampered by reduced markets.

Countermeasures the Shakers adopted to make their lifestyle more attractive had debatable results. Finally, federal and state laws hurt the Shakers, including the Pure Food and Drug Act of 1906, which restricted the sale of patent medicines, and laws which prohibited placement of orphans with religious societies.

In short, there were a variety of reasons for the Shaker decline. In 1974, when the bicentennial of Mother Ann's arrival in this country was being celebrated, only a dozen Shakers remained. There are even fewer now.

The last decade has been marked by disagreement over the future of the sect, with Canterbury resigned to the end of Shakerism in its traditional form and Sabbathday Lake determined to continue. The disagreement has moral, legal, and financial ramifications.

To understand recent differences, it is helpful to trace changes in Shaker administration. The central ministry shifted from New Lebanon with the closing of that community in the 1940s. In 1957, Eldress Frances Hall of Hancock, trustee, died. Her bank accounts were found to contain a large amount of money—rumored at more than $1 million—which represented revenue from the sale of various societies and other assets.

There was some sentiment for splitting the money among the remaining communities, but Parent Ministry Eldress Emma King of Canterbury consulted outsiders and it was decided in 1959 to deposit the funds in an account known as the Shaker Central Trust Fund, administered by the ministry and by attorneys.

In 1961, the last Shaker brother, Delmer Wilson, died. In August 1965, the ruling ministry, which then consisted of Eldresses Emma King and Marguerite Frost of Canterbury and Eldress Gertrude Soule of Sabbathday Lake, ordained that the society be closed to new members and that further recruiting cease.

The eldresses were quoted as agreeing with Elder Arthur Bruce, one of the last Shaker brethren, that as much bravery is required to walk through the end of an age as to found it.[1]

Complicating matters, however, was the presence at Sabbathday Lake of Theodore E. Johnson, who was appointed director of the community museum and library in 1960. Johnson expressed a desire to adopt the habits and beliefs of a Shaker. Sisters there eventually began to refer to him as "Brother Ted."

Meanwhile, the membership of the Parent Ministry changed again. Eldress Emma King died in 1966 and her place as a member of the Ministry was taken in 1967 by Eldress Bertha Lindsay of Canterbury. Eldress Marguerite Frost died in 1971, leaving the two present members of the Parent ministry, Eldress Gertrude Soule of Sabbathday and Eldress Bertha. Eldress Gertrude, growing uncomfortable at Sabbathday Lake, moved to Canterbury.

The Canterbury ministry became increasingly adamant about not admitting new members, and refused to recognize Mr. Johnson or any other recruits at Sabbathday Lake.

Canterbury still receives inquiries from persons who wish to start Shaker communities elsewhere. Persons in California and Iowa who expressed an interest were sent information. But, in the words of Eldress Bertha—quoting Mother Ann Lee—"new bees do not return to old hives."[2]

Eldress Bertha rejects the claims of Sabbathday Lake's few Shaker males: "There are no Shaker brothers," she says, asserting that since the sisters never had anything to do with the brothers' instruction, there was no one to instruct such men.

Canterbury's assets were turned over to a nonprofit corporation in 1973, under the direction of a thirty-two member board of trustees, to insure the preservation of the Shaker village. The directors included the eldresses as well as lay experts on Shaker life.

The disagreement that has occurred between Sabbathday Lake and Canterbury, involving both distribution of money from the central trust and the closing of membership, has so far detracted little from the apparent tranquility of the two villages or the tourist lure that each exerts.

Canterbury is visited by more than 16,000 persons yearly, though nestled off the mainstream of White Mountain tourist traffic eleven miles north of the state capital at Concord, New Hampshire. Eldresses Bertha and Gertrude traditionally greet the stream of visitors personally. For many years the burden of management of the museum and its guided programs was assumed by Charles F. "Bud" Thompson, once a folksinger and native of Roslindale, Massachusetts, who came to Canterbury in 1958 in search of Shaker music and stayed on as assistant to the eight ladies then resident.

Canterbury's most valued artifacts are housed in the white clapboard former meeting house built in 1792. The gift shop is located on the first floor of the trustees' office. A sitting room on that floor shows how Victorian and modern influences have affected the Shaker lifestyle. The room is furnished with easy chairs, an upright piano, a television set, and a patterned rug. The walls are papered.

Although the sisters have accepted invitations to travel on special occasions—as in the spring of 1975 when Harvard's Holy Hill was rededicated—their ages finally curtailed the scope of their travels. Sunday Sabbath is observed by listening to such commentators as Oral Roberts and Dr. Robert Schuler.

Sabbathday Lake is perhaps more representative of what life in a Shaker village once was like. The community is the residence of both men and women whose ages and numbers still permit at least a semblance of communal self-sufficiency. It conducts summer Sabbath services in the same meeting house built in 1794 by Moses Johnson, services characterized by simplicity and dignity, and—to the disappointment of some of the curious—entirely lacking frenzied protestations described as typical of earliest services. Sabbathday Lake's barn still shelters sheep, and some fields are under cultivation. The society produces herbal teas, culinary herbs, herbal vinegars, honey, and Shaker rosewater, selling these directly to visitors and by mail order. A few articles woven and knitted by the sisters are also sold.

Sabbathday Lake attracted sixty visitors when it first welcomed tourists in 1931. More than 5,000 persons now tour the complex each year. The Shaker property includes a summer place on the lake, which the sisters have little time to use because of the demands of the tourist season. Able-bodied sisters and volunteer friends take turns in staffing the gift shop.

The Shakers regularly alternate domestic chores, as always, each taking a turn in the kitchen. At a typical Saturday luncheon repast, the bell sounds for the noon meal. The few men assemble in the brothers' waiting room and the sisters in theirs. At the ringing of the second bell, men and women file into the dining area and take places at separate tables, standing for silent grace. Seated, the Shakers are served by two sisters "four to a square"—that is, family style to four diners. A simple menu might consist of home-baked beans, hot dogs, potato salad, fresh rolls and homemade bread, tea, and squash pie. Conversation is subdued but natural, including whatever visitors are present.

The dining area is located on the basement level of the dwelling house. Furniture consists of traditional trestle tables and ladderback chairs. The kitchen area still retains a tin sink and various china cupboards; the dinnerware is English porcelain in a cranberry and white pattern. The sisters wear calico print dresses with shawl collars and yokes. Most wear handknitted cardigan sweaters.

Theodore Johnson is one of Sabbathday Lake's more articulate spokesmen as well as being a key figure in the disagreement over the closing of the Shaker membership. Reared as an Episcopalian, Johnson was graduated from Colby College in 1953. He obtained a master's degree at Harvard in 1955 and was a student at the Harvard Divinity School from 1955 to 1957 and a Fulbright Scholar. He served a stint as a public librarian, became associated with the now defunct Bliss College, formerly of Lewiston, Maine, and has conducted Shaker study courses for Colby College, the University of Maine, and other institutions. He has served as director of the Sabbathday Lake museum since 1960 and presides over the community library.

Johnson is a busy man, as the community depends on him for its operations and upkeep. Alternately attired in dungaree coveralls, traditional Shaker smock, or street clothes, he fills roles as herbgrower, shepherd, farmer, librarian, village greeter, guide, and museum spokesman. He often uses the Biblical *yea* and *nay*.

Johnson dismisses the importance of his uncovenanted status. "There are Shakers buried there," he says, motioning toward the village cemetery, "who never signed a covenant." Johnson appears to have the support of the Sabbathday Lake sisters, including Sister R. Mildred Barker, an articulate speaker for the society through articles in the *Shaker Quarterly* and other publications. Sister Frances Carr, the youngest Shaker sister, also endorses Johnson's Shaker status and argues that the doors of any church should not be closed to anybody.

The issue of Shaker continuity is also complicated by various legendary prophecies. It is said that Mother Ann predicted a time when there would not be enough Shakers left to bury their dead, and an eventual rebirth of the faith. Another version predicts a rebirth when the number of Shakers declined to the number of the original mission. Mother Ann is quoted as saying, "If there is but one called out of a generation, and that soul is faithful, it will have to travail and bear for all its generation; for the world will be redeemed by generations."[3]

The Sabbathday Lake Shakers in recent years issued a statement echoing that thought. "For some years," they said, "it has been fashionable in some quarters to look upon Shakerism as dead. Let this serve as our assurance that it is not. Our Blessed Mother taught that salvation unto souls comes by generations and that so long as one person in a generation had the saving inner knowledge of the Gospel the work would go on. Although few in number it is our resolution that we be caught up more and more in the blessed work of God. We pray that with heavenly Guidance we may so make ourselves instruments of divine truth and light that the way of Believers may once again appear to the children of God as a meaningful, vital and challenging way of life. We solemnly commit ourselves to the task of so fanning the flame of Mother's Gospel that as this new decade which is now opening draws to its close we may see that Christ our Savior is indeed creating all things anew and that the Testimony shines forth more brightly than at any other time in this century."[4]

Shaker Anna White predicted in 1905 that "conditions suited to the needs of the new age will develop and take on form. The Shaker faith and the Shaker life, will, from its elastic nature, be ready to receive the impress of newly revealed truth and expand in new forms."[5]

Another view of the Shaker future was expressed in a commemorative speech at the Shaker bicentennial observance at Canterbury. Father Robley Edward Whitson, president of the United Institute, an ecumenical study center in Bethlehem, Connecticut, spoke of the trend towards ecumenical union. "In this new opening of Christian Unity," he said, "the Shaker Way of Life in Christ reaches out beyond its first forms to contribute its Gifts to the growing heritage we seek to share together. The Shaker Way is destined not to be lost, but to be an integral part of the transformation sweeping the Universal Church."[6]

Whatever the impact of these views and speculations,

Shakerism offers much to dwell upon for the present-day scholar. In addition to a vast body of literature, there are scores of Shaker attractions to visit and artifacts to inspect.

The most impressive restored village in the Northeast is that bordering Pittsfield, Massachusetts, at the site of the Hancock Shaker Village. Surviving buildings have been completely refurbished since the rundown village was saved as a museum in 1960 and furnished with a substantial collection of artifacts donated by the Edward Deming Andrewses. Besides the original Shirley meeting house, the most noticeable structure at Hancock is the so-called Round Stone Barn, which has an ell housing a permanent exhibit on Shaker agriculture. Visitors to Hancock can easily spend a half day touring the grounds and buildings.

Only four miles from Hancock, just across the New York state border, is the former motherhouse of the Order of Mount Lebanon, now the Darrow School, an independent secondary boarding school for boys and girls. Although a private institution, it preserves original Shaker buildings.

Nearby, housed in Shaker buildings of the Mount Lebanon South Family that were formerly used in the manufacture of chairs, are followers of Sufism, an Eastern sect derived from Moslem mysticism and incorporating elements of many religions. Numbering more than one hundred men, women, and children, this communal group of Sufis, though not celibate, feels that its philosophy corresponds in some ways to that of the Shakers, and even hints that the sect may be the fruition of Mother Ann's prophecy that Shakers will return in a new form.

The original Shaker community of Niskayuna—later known as Watervliet—is now geographically segmented as the community of Colonie, a suburb of Albany, New York; the balance of its acreage is incorporated into the Albany airport. Still surviving, however, in the shadow of the jetport, is the Shaker cemetery in which can be found the burial places of Mother Ann, William Lee, Lucy Wright and other early Shakers.[7] The society's original buildings are either privately owned or are part of the Ann Lee County Home.

Kentucky has two active Shaker sites of interest. The former

Pleasant Hill community, known now as Shakertown, is impressively restored to its early nineteenth century appearance and offers food and lodging to visitors in original buildings. Shakertown at South Union, Kentucky features an annual outdoor drama festival in early July that tells in song and dance the history of the South Union community from 1807 to 1922. One of the original buildings is part of St. Mark's Benedictine Priory.

Many museums, including those at Fruitlands, at the Winterthur Museum in Delaware, and at the artifact-loaded Shaker Museum in Old Chatham, New York, have libraries preserving church records, imprints, and manuscripts. New York's Metropolitan Museum of Art has a permanent exhibit, largely donated by the Andrews family, in its American wing. The museum at Old Chatham publishes a complete list of Shaker attractions throughout the country, on which the list in the appendix to this book is based.

The Andrews collection also furnished a Shaker room in the American Museum in Bath, England, a reminder that it was in England that Shakerism began. Shaker scholars have retraced the footsteps of Ann Lee's girlhood in England, finding only sparse evidence to either substantiate or dispute what has been called her "largely legendary biography."[8]

In assessing the life of Ann Lee and the history of Shakerism, both skepticism and faith distort the perception of the observer. Should Ann Lee be dismissed as an ignorant charismatic? Does her life reflect divine mission? Do her teachings imply inspired utterances, or are her words but the contrived fabrications of her apostles? What is the validity of her testament? Is Shakerism of one cloth or is it a fabric of constantly changing texture and design?

Historians are largely dependent on Shaker sources in recording Mother Ann's life. One such source, the 1905 book entitled *Shakerism: Its Meaning and Message*, contains an interesting anecdote that serves as a generational link between the life of Ann in England and that of her followers in America more than half a century later. "In the year 1838," the account states, "an English woman visiting [the Shaker community] at Alfred, Maine, remarked that she was from Manchester. Two Shaker sisters said, 'Why, that is where our Mother came from,' and proceeded to give some account of Ann Lee. The woman was greatly affected, and said with emotion: 'That is the very woman I have heard my mother talk about and cry as if her heart would break; she would give anything, to know what had become of that woman.' Her mother had been present when Ann Lee had been let out of the stone prison. A very great multitude had assembled to see her and were much affected by her appearance."[9] The account ends with the departing visitor excitedly determined to write her mother in England relating her great discovery.

There are other views besides those of the Shakers, some of them from chroniclers in Harvard and Shirley. Henry Nourse, in his *History of Harvard*, concluded an apparently straightforward description with a negative analysis: "The Shaker community, eliminating as it does all but the fraternal affections, and evading many social obligations and sympathies, can hardly be called a seminary of good citizenship." Nourse added, "It exerts little salutary influence beyond its own narrow limits." In Shirley, the Reverend Seth Chandler expressed a kindlier and simpler view, calculated perhaps to maintain harmony with his neighboring denomination: "From a long and intimate acquaintance with this peculiar people," Chandler wrote, "the compiler has been led to regard them as a sincere and devoted band of Christian brethren, who are seeking a better country, that is a heavenly."[10]

Edward Deming Andrews, reviewing controversial aspects of Ann Lee and the Shaker faith, wrote that these considerations should not "obscure the fact that she instituted a movement deeply religious in aspiration and essentially democratic in practice. Her advocacy of equal rights (and responsibilities) for women in the Shaker society anticipated the feminist movement in America. Her belief in an equalitarian order, in the dignity of labor, and in the rights of conscience accorded with American idealism. Principles such as these spoken with what seemed to her followers like divine authority, inspired them in their efforts to establish a truly Christian community, in many respects the most successful experiment in religious communitarianism in American history."[11]

An article by C. Allyn Russell in a New York state history periodical cites many of the same contributions cataloged by Andrews, as well as "their unique acceptance of the Negro on equal terms." On the negative side, however, Russell asserts that "scholars will point to their failure to appreciate the sacramental nature of marriage; their legalism which smothered much natural development; and their autocratic polity which subtly created a 'ruling' and a 'ruled' class." Russell sums up the ambivalent judgment that builds among critics, perceiving a "curious combination of regimentation and individuality, of demonstrative expression and orderly tranquillity, of separation from the world and contact with it, of monkish asceticism and mundane delight, of sexuality and sexual segregation, of autocracy and democracy, of persecution and recognition."[12]

The Shaker heritage is increasingly being evaluated in light of contemporary values. Concerns such as the dangers of additives and chemicals in food products, the reexamination of the inevitability of war, and the unequal treatment of the races and sexes, have brought new attention to Shaker opinions on these matters. A trustee of the Darrow School at New Lebanon wrote in the school magazine of his view of Shaker relevance: "If you're an auto mechanic, stand for a clean running engine and for not bilking your customers," he said. "If you're a doctor, stand for a little extra caring. If you're a student, stand for not buying your term paper. Stand for the best hamburgers on the block. Stand for not wasting gas . . . ."[13]

Whatever people may think of the Shakers—even those who regard them as deluded—almost everyone seems to recognize their basic decency. Shaker student Tom Davenport captured the essential Shaker spirit when he observed, "I think there's something in us that will always love them. The idea of righteousness is a stronger current in our society than many people realize, and righteousness has always been pretty much the property of organized churches. To find a group of people who have been living righteousness for two hundred years instead of just talking about it is a rare and beautiful experience."[14]

Father Robley Whitson of the ecumenically oriented United

Institute sees Shakerism as "pouring out its gifts upon the world" in the movement toward worldwide Christian cooperation.[15] Citing an 1880 editorial on the union of churches, Whitson argues that Shakerism was in the vanguard of the ecumenical movement. Shakerism seems to have exerted a particular fascination among Roman Catholics, perhaps partly because three of the former Shaker villages were taken over by Catholic religious orders. The Alfred community in Maine became the site of a school run by the Brothers of Christian Instruction, the Enfield, New Hampshire community was acquired by the Missionaries of Our Lady of LaSalette, and South Union, Kentucky by the Benedictines.)

While Shakers themselves would like to be appreciated for their spiritual values, their cultural impact was considerable. It is apparent in Shaker crafts and furniture; the paintings of Charles Sheeler; the music of Aaron Copland; the Shaker dance choreographed by Martha Graham and Doris Humphrey; and the literature of two centuries, including works by Hawthorne and Howells and such contemporary novels as Janet Holt Giles's *The Believers* and Nancy Zaroulis's *Call the Darkness Light*. Shaker design in furniture is viewed at such auction houses as Sotheby Parke Bernet on New York's Madison Avenue, in reproductions of Shaker chairs, cabinets and other pieces, and in the documented debt of inspiration Danish modern design owes to the Shakers.

With all these reminders, it seems unlikely that Shakerism will soon be forgotten. The evidence of past glories is attracting an increasingly appreciative following. The impact that Shakers now living may have on the Shaker image is yet to be measured. But it can be predicted with some certainty that Mother Ann's spiritual message will continue to exert influence in a world full of seekers

---

A one-horse carriage approaches on Shaker Road past Church Family buildings in this turn-of-the-century photograph (opposite) *from a glass negative. Square House borders extreme left. Only the Second House, the most distant building, remains of those on the right. (Courtesy of Erhart Muller)*

alert to eternal truths and inspired wisdom. With Armageddon threatening modern civilization, Mother Ann's words to her followers now seem prophetic:[16] "Some of you think that you will yet subdue and overcome the nations of the earth; but you are mistaken: they have that work to do themselves. They will fight and devour and dash each other to pieces, until they become so humbled as to be willing to receive the gospel."

Guide to Shaker Museums, Collections, and Libraries

CONNECTICUT

Connecticut State Library, 231 Capitol Avenue, Hartford, 06115. Large collection of Enfield, Connecticut, miscellaneous pamphlets housed in rare and special books section. Tel. (203) 566-4777.

DELAWARE

The Henry Francis DuPont Winterthur Museum, Winterthur, 19735. Off Rte. 52. Two rooms of Shaker furnishings may be seen on museum tours, for which reservations are required. Museum library has collection of extremely rare and early Shaker books and manuscripts. The repository for much of the Andrews' collection. Tel. (302) 656-8591.

'This guide is adapted from the "Blue List" distributed by the Shaker Museum, Old Chatham, New York, 12136. For latest operating hours, fees, persons to contact, and other information, consult the revised list available at token cost from Old Chatham.

DISTRICT OF COLUMBIA

Library of Congress: Books in the general collection; special materials in the American Folklife Center and the Rare Book, Manuscript and Music Divisions. Tel. (202) 287-5000.

INDIANA

Indiana Historical Society Library, 315 West Ohio Street, Indianapolis, 46202. West Union (Busro) Material. Tel. (317) 633-4976.

KENTUCKY

Kentucky Museum, Bowling Green, 42101. Kentucky Building, U.S. Rte. 68 on Western Kentucky University campus. Collection of Kentucky material culture, including South Union Shaker furniture, tools and crafts. Library has Kentuckiana research collection, especially South Union Shaker manuscripts. Tel. (502) 745-2592.

Shakertown at Pleasant Hill, Inc., Harrodsburg, 40330. U.S. Rte. 68, 25 miles southwest of Lexington. A restored Shaker village, of which 27 original buildings remain; finest remaining Shaker site in the South. Dining and overnight lodgings available in original buildings. Tel. (606) 734-5411.

Shakertown at South Union, 42283. U.S. Rte. 68 and Ky. 73, 15 miles west of Bowling Green and 3 miles east of Auburn. A large collection of Shaker furniture, crafts and textiles, housed in the 1824 Centre House. Small but interesting library collection. Tel. (502) 542-4167.

Filson Club, 118 West Breckenridge Street, Louisville, 40203. Pleasant Hill Library material. Tel (502) 582-3727.

University of Kentucky, Margaret I. King Library, Lexington, 40406. Off Rose Street opposite Columbia Avenue. Most materials are in the Special Collections Department. Tel (606) 258-8611.

MAINE

Shaker Museum, Sabbathday Lake Shaker Community, 04274. Poland Spring, 23 miles north of Portland. Maine Turnpike (Interstate 95; toll) to Gray, Exit 11; north 8 miles on Rte. 26. An original Shaker village founded in 1793, still occupied by Shaker sisters. Gift shop open year round; museum, in summers. Extensive research library. Tel. (207) 926-4865.

MASSACHUSETTS

Boston Museum of Fine Arts, 465 Huntington Avenue, Back Bay, 02115. Shaker recreated room with furniture, artifacts. Tel. (617) 267-9300.

Fruitlands Museums, Prospect Hill, Harvard, 01451. Off Rte. 110 north of Harvard Common. Shaker museum is one of five collections on the grounds. Extensive library collection. Tel. (617) 456-3924.

Hancock Shaker Community, Inc., Hancock, 01201. U.S. Rte. 20, 5 miles west of Pittsfield. A former Shaker village, now under restoration; 17 original buildings, including famous Round Barn. Library materials. Tel. (413) 443-0188.

American Antiquarian Society, Worcester, 01609. 185 Salisbury Street, corner of Park Avenue. Tel. (617) 755-5221.

Berkshire Athenaeum, 1 Wendell Avenue, Pittsfield, 01201. Tel. (413) 442-1559.

Massachusetts Historical Society, Boston, 02215. 1154 Boylston Street. Tel. (617) 536-1608.

Williams College, Sawyer Library, Williamstown, 01267. Off Rte. 2, in center of campus. Tel. (413) 597-2502.

Shaker Holy Land, Harvard, 01451. P.O. Box 459. Information on Harvard and Shirley.

MICHIGAN

University of Michigan, William L. Clements Library, South University Avenue, Ann Arbor, 48109. Tel. (313) 764-2347.

NEW HAMPSHIRE

Canterbury Shaker Museum, East Canterbury, 03224. Located 13.5 miles northeast of Concord; U.S. Rtes. 4 and 202, 4 miles to Rte. 106; bear left 6.5 miles, then turn left on road marked 'Shaker Village' three miles. An original Shaker village founded in 1792, still occupied by Shaker sisters. Gift Shop and tours. Tel. (603) 783-9822.

New Hampshire Historical Society Library, Concord, 03301. 30 Park Street, behind State House. Tel. (603) 225-3381.

NEW YORK

Shaker Museum, Old Chatham, 12136. Near Exit B-2 of the N.Y. Thruway (Berkshire Spur); 20 miles SE of Albany off U.S. Rte. 20, turn south on Rte. 66 and follow signs. Exhibit buildings and gift shop. Emma B. King Library. Tel. (518) 794-9100.

Buffalo and Erie County Public Library, Buffalo, 14203. Lafayette Square. Rare Book Room. Tel. (716) 856-7525 Ext. 244.

Hofstra University Library, Hemstead, Long Island, 11550. 1000 Fulton Avenue. Special Collections, 9th floor. Tel. (516) 560-3440.

Metropolitan Museum of Art, New York City, 10028. Fifth Avenue at 82nd Street. Shaker Retiring Room, furnished largely from the Andrews' collection. On permanent exhibit in the American Wing. Tel. (212) 879-5500.

New York Public Library, New York City, 10018. Fifth Avenue at 42nd Street. Special Collections: Manuscript and Archives Division. Tel. (212) 790-6254

New York State Library, Albany, 12230. Cultural Education Center, The Governor Nelson A. Rockefeller Empire State Plaza. Tel. (518) 474-5161.

Syracuse University, George Arents Research Library, Syracuse, 13210. Tel. (315) 423-2585.

NORTH CAROLINA

Duke University, William R. Perkins Library, Durham, 27706. Tel. (919) 684-2947.

OHIO

Dunham Tavern Museum, Cleveland, 44106. 6709 Euclid Avenue. One room furnished in Shaker furniture. Tel. (216) 431-1060.

Golden Lamb Hotel, Lebanon, 45036. 27–31 South Broadway, on Rte. 63 between I–71 and I–75. Ohio's oldest hostelry. Hotel is richly furnished with antiques, many Shaker. Authentic Shaker bedroom and Shaker Goodroom (pantry). Shaker dining room for the public. Tel. (513) 932-5065

Kettering–Moraine Museum, Kettering, 45439. 35 Moraine Circle South, West Stroop Street and Kettering Boulevard. Three Shaker rooms dedicated to the Watervliet, Ohio Shaker Community. Tel. (513) 299-2722; if no answer, (513) 299-0594.

Shaker Historical Society Museum, Shaker Heights, 44120. 16740 South Park Boulevard. Exhibits mainly from North Union. Some manuscripts. Tel. (216) 921-1201.

Warren County Historical Society Museum, Lebanon, 45036. 105 South Broadway on Rte. 63 between I–71 and I–75; two doors south of the Golden Lamb Hotel. Shaker furniture and crafts. Research collection. Tel. (513) 932-1817.

Western Reserve Historical Society, History Museum, Cleveland, 44106. 10825 East Boulevard. Shaker exhibit. Largest research collection of Shakeriana in the world. The collection is available on microfilm. Tel. (216) 721-5722.

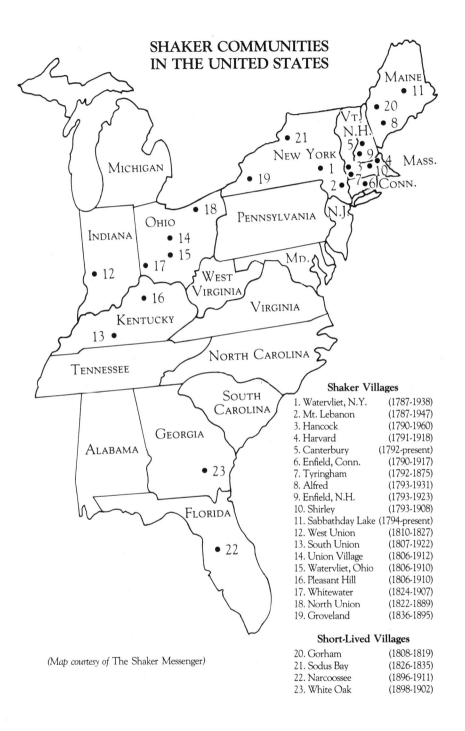

SHAKER COMMUNITIES
IN THE UNITED STATES

Shaker Villages

1. Watervliet, N.Y.   (1787-1938)
2. Mt. Lebanon   (1787-1947)
3. Hancock   (1790-1960)
4. Harvard   (1791-1918)
5. Canterbury   (1792-present)
6. Enfield, Conn.   (1790-1917)
7. Tyringham   (1792-1875)
8. Alfred   (1793-1931)
9. Enfield, N.H.   (1793-1923)
10. Shirley   (1793-1908)
11. Sabbathday Lake (1794-present)
12. West Union   (1810-1827)
13. South Union   (1807-1922)
14. Union Village   (1806-1912)
15. Watervliet, Ohio   (1806-1910)
16. Pleasant Hill   (1806-1910)
17. Whitewater   (1824-1907)
18. North Union   (1822-1889)
19. Groveland   (1836-1895)

Short-Lived Villages

20. Gorham   (1808-1819)
21. Sodus Bay   (1826-1835)
22. Narcoossee   (1896-1911)
23. White Oak   (1898-1902)

(Map courtesy of The Shaker Messenger*)*

Dayton and Montgomery County Public Library, Dayton, 45402. 215 East 3rd Street. Tel. (513) 224-1651.

Ohio Historical Society Library, Columbus, 43211. I–71 and 17th Avenue. Tel. (614) 466-1500 Ext. 326.

PENNSYLVANIA

Philadelphia Museum of Art, 19130. Benjamin Franklin Parkway at 26th Street. Exhibit of Shaker furniture and artifacts. Complete Sister's room from New Lebanon Center. Tel. (215) 763–8100.

VERMONT

Shelburne Museum, 05482. U.S. Rte. 7, seven miles south of Burlington. Shaker artifacts in Shaker shed from Canterbury, New Hampshire. Tel. (802) 985–3344.

WISCONSIN

Milwaukee Art Center: Villa Terrace, 53202. 2220 North Terrace Avenue. Tel. (414) 271–3565.

State Historical Society of Wisconsin, Madison, 53706. 816 State Street. Tel. (608) 262–9590.

ENGLAND

The American Museum in Britain, Claverton Manor, Bath, BA2 7BD. Train from London, 1¼ hour; 2½ miles from the center of Bath. Twenty galleries of Americana, including a Shaker room furnished from the Andrews' collection. Tel. Bath 60503. Education Tel. 63538.

Notes

Chapter 2: From Lancashire to America

1. Charles Dickens, *Hard Times* (New York: Heritage Press), p. 2.
2. William E. A. Axon, ed., *Lancashire Gleanings* (Manchester, England: Tubbs, Brook & Crystal, 1883), pp. 79–84.
3. Calvin Green and Seth Y. Wells, *A Summary View of the Millennial Church or United Society of Believers, Commonly Called Shakers, Comprising the Rise, Progress and Practical Order of the Society together with the General Principles of their Faith and Testimony* (Albany, 1823), p.6.
4. Toad Lane was originally rural in character. The name may have referred to the toads that lived along the lane or it could be a corruption of "the old lane." It may also have been a corruption of Tod Lane, a spelling which appeared in one old record. If so, the name may have referred to foxes rather than toads. Modern Todd Street is near Victoria Station.
5. Rufus Bishop and Seth Y. Wells, *Testimonies of the Life, Character, Revelations and Doctrines of Mother Ann Lee, and the Elders with Her, through Whom the World of Eternal Life, Was Opened in this*

*Day of Christ's Second Appearing, Collected from Living Witnesses, in Union with the Church . . .,*2nd ed. (Albany, New York: Weed, Parsons, & Co., Pri..ters, 1888), p. 2. Ann seems to have had from her earliest years a talent for incurring the wrath of those around her. One of her brothers became so enraged at her as she sat singing that he grabbed a stick the size of a "broom handle" and beat her over the head and face until the stick splintered. See Anna White and Leila S. Taylor, *Shakerism, Its Meaning and Message* (North Family of Shakers, Mount Lebanon, New York, 1904), p. 23. Assuming the beating by her brother took place, this could partly explain skull fractures observed when Mother Ann's remains were moved in 1835.

6. Green, *Summary View*, p. 6.
7. *Ibid.*
8. *Ibid.*, p. 5. Daniel Patterson states that "any direct historical relationship is doubtful and is certainly yet to be proved." He said that confusion resulted because lay scholars uncritically read Benjamin S. Youngs's book *Testimony of Christ's Second Appearing*. See Daniel Patterson, *The Shaker Spiritual* (Princeton, New Jersey: Princeton University Press, 1979), p. xv.
9. Bishop, *Testimonies*, p. 50. Among the places Whitefield preached in America was the town of Harvard. He was banned from preaching by a number of pastors, including those in Harvard's neighboring communities of Groton, Littleton, Lunenburg and Leominster. See Samuel Abbott Green's *The Natural History and the Topography of Groton, Massachusetts . . .* (Cambridge, Mass.: University Press, 1912), p. 155.
10. Benjamin Seth Youngs, *Testimony of Christ's Second Appearing, Exemplified by the Principles and Practice of the True Church of Christ. History of the Progressive Work of God, Extending from the Creation of Man to the "Harvest."—Comprising the Four Great Dispensations Now Comsummating in the Millennial Church. Antichrist's Kingdom, or Churches, Contrasted with the Church of Christ's First and Second Appearing, the Kingdom of God of Heaven,* 4th ed. (Albany, New York: Published by the United Society, Called Shakers, 1856), p. 210.

   An ecumenical spirit has evolved between Roman Catholics and the Shakers in the last few decades. Trappist monk and popular author Thomas Merton became an appreciator of the Shaker simplicity and dedication. In 1965, a gold medal was presented to the Shakers by the Catholic Art Association. The citation stated: "In the midst of a world in which commercial values were rapidly superceding religious ones, these devoted people demonstrated the practicality of the good life they had chosen. They resolved many of the problems that confront

industrial society today, and thus give hope that we, and other
followers of the Gospels, may see the achievement of equally successful
solutions." See *Shaker Quarterly*, Fall 1965, p. 102.

11. Green, *Summary View*, p. 9.
12. Axon, *Lancashire Gleanings*, pp. 85–86.
13. Green, *Summary View*, p. 12.
14. *Ibid.*
15. Edward Deming Andrews, *People Called Shakers* (New York: Dover
    Publications, 1963), p. 11.
16. Green, *Summary View*, p. 49.
17. *Ibid.*
18. *Ibid.*, p. 13.
19. *Ibid.*, p. 14.
20. Bishop, *Testimonies*, p. 35.
21. Green, *Summary View*, p. 15.
22. Edwin Scott Gaustad, *The Great Awakening in New England*
    (Chicago: Quadrangle Books, 1968), p. 27.
23. Bishop, *Testimonies*, p. 16.
24. Herbert A. Wisbey, Jr., "The Dark Day of 1780," *Yankee*, May 1965,
    p. 76.
25. Andrews, *People Called Shakers*, p. 21.
26. Green, *Summary View*, p. 25.
27. Seth Y. Wells, *Testimonies Concerning the Character and Ministry of
    Mother Ann Lee and the First Witnesses of the Gospel of Christ's Se-
    cond Appearing; Given by Some of the Aged Brethren and Sisters of
    the United Society, including a few sketches of their own religious ex-
    perience: Approved by the Church* (Albany, New York: printed by
    Packard & Van Benthuysen, 1827), p. 45.
28. *Ibid.*, p. 51.
29. There are also frequent references in early journals to Mother Ann's
    eyes and the power of her touch. This has given rise to purely
    speculative theories that Mother Ann had hypnotic powers. Clara
    Endicott Sears, a Shaker historian with an affinity for romance and
    mysticism, alluded to these accounts in a paper delivered at a meeting
    of the Bay State Historical League in the Harvard Unitarian Church,
    Harvard, Mass., on July 22, 1939. She drew attention to "the very
    striking fact that in each case Mother Ann either laid her hand on their
    arms or on their shoulders. Anyone knowing anything about the
    methods used in hypnotism," Miss Sears ventured, "will recognize the
    fact that Mother Ann all unconsciously used the same methods."
30. Wells, *Testimonies Concerning the Character*, p. 105.
31. *Ibid.*, p. 51.
32. *Ibid.*, p. 77.

33. *Ibid.*
34. *Ibid.*, p. 85.
35. *Ibid.*, p. 74.
36. Mother Ann's travels took her to Enfield, Preston, Stafford, Stonington, and Windham in Connecticut, and Ashfield, Belchertown, Cheshire, Grafton, Granby, Hancock, Montague, Mt. Washington, Norton, Petersham, Rehoboth, Richmond, Shelburne, and Upton in Massachusetts.

Chapter 3: Harvard and Shirley

1. Elvira L. Scorgie, "Harvard 1732," in *Towns of the Nashaway Plantation* (Hudson: Lancaster League of Historical Societies, 1976), p. 46.
2. Henry S. Nourse, *History of the Town of Harvard, Massachusetts 1732–1893* (Harvard: Printed for Warren Hapgood, 1894), p. 256.
3. Nourse, *History of Harvard*, p. 255.
4. John B. Willard, "Old Places and Houses in Harvard, "*Turner's Public Spirit*, 18 March 1876.
5. *The Manifesto*, December 1899, p. 287.
6. Nourse, *History of Harvard*, p. 255.
7. Clara Endicott Sears, comp., *Gleanings from Old Shaker Journals* (Boston: Houghton Mifflin Co., 1916), p. 4.
8. *Manifesto*, December 1899, p. 287. The cornfield where Ireland was buried was located just to the east of the Shaker office building. John B. Willard, who served on the Harvard School Committee with Elder Elijah Myrick cites this location in the book *Picturesque Worcester*, p. 86.
9. *Manifesto*, December 1899, p. 288.
10. Green, *Summary View*, p. 20.
11. Willard, "Old Places," *Public Spirit*, 18 March 1876.
12. Bishop, *Testimonies*, p. 67.
13. Sears, *Gleanings*, p. 37.
14. *Ibid.*, p. 38.
15. Nourse, *History of Harvard*, p. 258. The sale price is alternately expressed as $1,666.67 and the deed was dated April 29, 1782.
16. Wells, *Testimonies Concerning the Character*, p. 62.
17. Bishop, *Testimonies*, p. 176.
18. Valentine Rathbun, *Some Brief Hints of a Religious Scheme* (Salem: Reprinted and Sold by S. Hall, 1782), p. 12.
19. Amos Taylor, *Narrative of the Strange Principles, Conduct and Character of the People Known by the Name of Shakers* (Worcester, 1782), p. 15.
20. William Plumer, "The Original Shaker Communities in New England," *The New England Magazine*, Boston, May 1900, pp. 304–6.

21. Nourse, *History of Harvard*, p. 259.
22. Bishop, *Testimonies*, p. 70.
23. *Ibid.*, p. 79.
24. Nelde K. Drumm and Margaret P. Harley, *Lunenburg: The Heritage of Turkey Hills 1718-1978* (Leominster: Lunenburg Historical Society, 1977), p. 55.
25. Bishop, *Testimonies*, p. 87.
26. Green, *Summary View*, p. 163.
27. Bishop, *Testimonies*, p. 87.
28. *Ibid.*, p. 89.
29. *Ibid.*, p. 92.
30. *Ibid.*, p. 94.
31. *Ibid.*, p. 98
32. *Ibid.*
33. Green, *Summary View*, p. 21. Some of the Shaker tormentors in the Harvard bishopric had financial reverses; one committed suicide; another's house burned down; still another developed a shaking disease which caused general disability, including sexual impotency. "Thus he became a Shaker in judgment," the believers commented (see Bishop, *Testimonies*, p. 299). Phineas Farnworth, Jonathan Houghton and Asa Houghton, and Jacob Whitney had financial problems; Farnworth and Joseph Houghton reportedly came to the Shakers to beg for charity. Whitney, the town clerk, was accused of having exacted fines from the Shaker leaders.

    The Shakers said that the town of Petersham was cursed. The growth of Petersham was stunted in the mid–1840s by three "catastrophes." Two fires wiped out fourteen buildings in the center of town, and the railroad by-passed the town seven miles to the north. Though these events combined to stagnate Petersham's economy, the rural town remains one of the prettiest in Massachusetts and the populace might well argue that the town is blessed, not cursed.
34. Bishop, *Testimonies*, p. 115.
35. *Ibid.*
36. *Ibid.*, p. 117.
37. According to White and Taylor, "It is a fact of local history that the tree to which Father James was tied soon after died." *Shakerism, Its Meaning and Message*, p. 52.
38. Bishop, *Testimonies*, p. 119.
39. *Ibid.*, p. 120.
40. *Ibid.*
41. *Ibid.*
42. *Ibid.*, p. 158.
43. Green, *Summary View*, p. 41.
44. Bishop, *Testimonies*, p. 274.

45. *Ibid.*
46. Green, *Summary View*, p. 37.
47. Joel Munsell, *Annals of Albany*, 2d ed. (Albany: J. Munsell, 1869), 2:288.

Chapter 4: The Gathering

1. Bishop, *Testimonies*, p. 290.
2. Andrews, *People Called Shakers*, p. 50.
3. Joseph Meacham, *A Concise Statement of the Principles of the Only True Church, According to the Gospel of the Present Appearance of Christ . . . Together with a Letter from James Whittaker, Minister of the Gospel in this day of Christ's Second Appearing—to his natural Relations in England.* Dated October 9th, 1785 (Bennington, Vermont: Haswell & Russell, 1790), p. 12.
4. Thomas Brown, *An Account of the People Called Shakers* (Troy, New York: Parker and Bliss, 1812), p. 331.
5. Bishop, *Testimonies*, p. 281.
6. *Ibid.*, p. 285.
7. Green, *Summary View*, p. 47.
8. D. Hamilton Hurd, comp., *History of Middlesex County, Massachusetts, with Biographical Sketches of Many of its Pioneers and Prominent Men* (Philadelphia: J.W. Lewis & Co., 1890), 2:873.
9. Mona M. Piotrowski, in *The Challenge of Change* Ruth Bridge, ed. (Enfield, Conn.: Enfield Historical Society, 1977), p. 34.
10. Bishop, *Testimonies*, p. 172.
11. Seth Chandler, *History of the Town of Shirley: From its Earliest Settlement to AD 1882* (Published by the author, 1883), p. 269.
12. Bishop, *Testimonies*, p. 224.
13. Nourse, *History of Harvard*, p. 254.
14. *Ibid.*, p. 268.
15. Shaker history records a conversation between Mother Ann and Lafayette, but the date of his actual visit is believed to have been three weeks after Mother Ann's death.
16. Anna White and Leila S. Taylor, *Shakerism, Its Meaning and Message* (North Family of Shakers, Mount Lebanon, New York, 1904), p. 178.
17. Ethel Stanwood Bolton, *Shirley Uplands and Intervales: Annals of a Border Town of Middlesex* (Boston: G.E. Littlefield, 1914), p. 183.
18. Nourse, *History of Harvard*, p. 145.
19. "Manifest Journal, 1791–1806," manuscript in Fruitlands Museums, Harvard, Mass.
20. Bolton, *Shirley Uplands*, pp. 186–87.
21. "Manifest Journal, 1791–1806," Fruitlands Museums.
22. *The Diary of William Bentley, D.D., Pastor of the East Church, Salem, Massachusetts* (Salem: The Essex Institute, 1907), 2:150.

23. *Ibid.*, p. 152.
24. Youngs, *Testimony of Christ's Second Appearing*, p. 630.

Chapter 5: Millennial Church

1. Green, *Summary View*, p. 163.
2. Wells, *Testimonies*, p. 37.
3. R.W. Pelham, *A Shaker's Answer to the Oft-Repeated Question, What Would Become of the World if All Should Become Shakers?"* (Boston: Rand, Avery & Co., 1874), p. 2.
4. Bishop, *Testimonies*, p. 208.
5. Green, *Summary View*, p. 31.
6. Green, *Summary View*, p. 38. Did the Shakers consider Mother Ann the second Christ? The official name of the group—the United Society of Believers in Christ's Second Appearing—and the contention that Mother Ann was the female manifestation of the Christ spirit implies that Ann was the Messiah reborn.

   One Shaker source asserted, "This extraordinary female, whom her followers believe God had chosen, and in whom Christ did visibly make his second appearance, was Ann Lee." But a clarifying footnote states, "It was the *Christ*, not Jesus who should make a second appearance." (Bishop, *Testimonies*, p. 2.)

   Such interpretation is rejected in an 1859 Shaker text which states, "It is no longer believed that Ann Lee was a 'witch' because she was known to possess supernatural powers; or that the Shakers think her to be something more than human—equal to Christ; or that they worship her, etc., etc." See Frederick W. Evans, *Shakers: Compendium of the Origin, History, Principles, Rules and Regulations, Governments, and Doctrines of the United Society of Believers in Christ's Second Appearing, with Biographies of Ann Lee, William Lee, Jas. Whittaker, J. Hocknell, J. Meacham, and Lucy Wright (New York: Lenox Hill Pub. & Dist. Co.* Burt Franklin 1972 reprint of 1859 publication), p. VI.

   A modern statement of principles maintains the following: "We recognize the Christ Spirit, the expression of Deity, first manifested in its fullness in Jesus of Nazareth. We also regard Ann Lee as the first to receive in this latter day the interior realization that the same Divine Spirit which was in Jesus might dwell within the consciousness of any man, woman, or child." See Eldress M. Catharine Allen, *The American Shakers* (Sabbathday Lake, Maine; The United Society, 1974), p. 3.

7. Bishop, *Testimonies*, p. 210.
8. *Ibid.*
9. *Ibid.*, p. 273.
10. *Ibid.*, p. 245.

11. *Ibid.*, p. 219.

12. *Ibid.*, p. 220.

13. Arthur F. Joy, *The Queen of the Shakers* (Minneapolis: T.S. Denison & Co., Inc., 1960), p. 125

14. Chandler, *History of Shirley*, p. 274.

15. Sears, *Gleanings*, p. 191.

16. Allen Chamberlain, *Annals of the Grand Monadnock*, 3rd. ed. (Concord, N.H.; Society for the Protection of New Hampshire Forests, 1975), p. 165.

17. Nourse, *History of Harvard*, p. 270.

18. Hurd, *History of Middlesex County*, p. 666

19. Besides Mother Hannah, the Harvard Shaker Cemetery was the final resting place of Mother Sarah Kendal of the Alfred, Maine, society, who died at Harvard in 1852.

20. Green, *Summary View*, p. 35.

21. Bates almost literally trailed the footsteps of another planter, John Chapman, whose planting of the appleseed in the newly populated Ohio Valley during the same decade became part of the national folklore. It is a coincidence that these two men, whose careers should be so closely parallel, would have roots that nearly intertwined in central Massachusetts. Chapman was born and reared in Leominster and set out amidst the Westward migration, establishing orchards along the Ohio River; Bates was spiritually nurtured in New England, ministering to the Shaker colonies of Harvard and Shirley before setting forth to plant the gospel of Mother Ann.

22. The Shakers also issued a disclaimer of sorts about radical behavior in the early church, explaining that "the work was all new to those who embraced it, and the leaders being few in number, and the work extensive, irregularities could not always be forseen nor prevented." See Green, *Summary View*, p. 18.

23. Roxalana L. Grosvenor, *The Shaker Covenant* (Boston: W.C. Allan, Printer, 1873), p. 11.

24. "Rules and Orders 1860," pp. 55, 56, manuscript in Fruitlands Museums, Harvard, Mass.

25. *Ibid.*

26. Green, *Summary View*, 2nd ed. rev. and impr., republished by the United Society, with the Approbation of the Ministry. (Albany, N.Y.: Printed by C. Van Benthuysen, 1848), p. 73.

27. Joseph Hammond, "Account of the Shakers," in Spofford, Jeremiah, *A Gazetteer of Massachusetts* (Newburyport, Mass., 1828), p. 273.

28. Nourse, *History of Harvard*, p. 455.

29. Philemon Stewart's *A Holy, Sacred, and Divine Roll and Book*, which was printed at Canterbury, New Hampshire, in 1843, was bound in the community at Harvard. The 500 copies were distributed to the

governors of the United States, to foreign missions, and to European governments. The most important publication to be printed at Harvard was William Leonard's book on community economy.

Chapter 6: Mother's Work

1. White and Taylor, *Shakerism*, p. 321.
2. George Holyoake, *The History of Cooperation in England; Its Literature and its Advocates* 3rd ed. (London: Trubner and Co., 1885), 2:290-91.
3. Mrs. Bolton, in her history of Shirley, related that the only Negro Shakeress in the community was Chloe Harris, actually a mulatto, being the daughter of a black man from Lunenburg and a white woman from Shirley.
4. Edward Wagenknecht, ed., *Mrs. Longfellow: Selected Letters and Journals of Fanny Appleton Longfellow* (New York: Longmans, Green and Co., 1956), p. 62.
5. Andrews, *People*, pp. 156-57.
6. Sears, *Gleanings*, p. 210.
7. *Ibid.*
8. *Ibid.*, p. 243.
9. Abijah Perkins Marvin, *History of the Town of Lancaster, Massachusetts, from the First Settlement to the Present Time, 1643-1879* (Lancaster: Published by the Town, 1879), pp. 371-73.
10. In 1847, Harvard and Shirley Shakers began hearing about a new wave of spiritualism among the world's people. Two young girls, Margaret and Kate Fox, were the instruments of this phenomenon. The Fox sisters, who lived in upstate New York, testified that they heard mysterious rapping sounds, and that by replicating the sounds they entered into communication with the spirit world, particularly with a man alleged to have been murdered in their home years earlier. The girls extracted detailed information from their spirit contacts by using a series of rapping noises coupled with alphabetical and numerical codes and simple yes and no responses. The "Rochester Knockings," as they came to be called, touched off an epidemic of spiritualistic fervor in America. It was estimated that there were some thirty thousand mediums practicing throughout the country within a few years. See R. M. Devens, *Our First Century* (Springfield, Mass.: C. A. Nichols & Co., 1880), p. 475.

  The Fox sisters were aptly named. One of the sisters admitted some forty years later that they contrived the rappings as a prank on their superstitious mother.

  Although Shaker spiritualism peaked in the era of Mother Ann's Work, and despite the skepticism that must have developed with the revelation of the Fox sister's deception, Shakers maintained belief in spirit communication. As late as the 1880s, the Shaker sisters in Harvard customarily gathered in their rooms during long winter evenings, and–joining hands while seated in a circle–would receive from a medium among them communication from the departed. See Arthur T. West, "Reminiscences of Life in a Shaker Village," *New England Quarterly*, June 1938, p. 349.

11. Clara Endicott Sears, comp., *Bronson Alcott's Fruitlands* (Boston: Houghton Mifflin Co., 1915), pp. 45–46.
12. Odell Shepard, ed., *Journals of A.B. Alcott* (Boston: Little, Brown & Co., 1938), p. 153.
13. Charles Lane, "A Day With the Shakers," *Dial*, October 1843, p. 167.
14. Sears, *Fruitlands*, p. 120.
15. "The Shakers," *Literary Souvenir*, V.3, April 10, 1841, pp. 116–17.
16. "Charles Lane and the Shakers," *The Regenerator*, February 8, 1847, p. 358.
17. Sears, *Gleanings*, p. 244.
18. *Ibid.*, p. 245.
19. *Ibid.*, p. 246.
20. *Ibid.*, p. 245.

Chapter 7: Prosperity and Personality

1. "Shirley Records, 1842–1858," Harvard (Mass.) Historical Society.
2. Sears, *Gleanings*, p. 222.
3. *Ibid.*, pp. 249–50.
4. Andrews, *People*, p. 114.
5. Luther Burbank, the most famous of early American horticulturists, spent his boyhood within walking distance of the Shaker villages of Harvard and Shirley and competed with them in the marketplace. Original and practical in his methods of raising seeds, he produced quality vegetables and had them ready for the Fitchburg market earlier than other gardeners, thus securing the highest prices. He moved to California in 1875, having already developed the Burbank potato. He ultimately developed 250 varieties of fruit, flowers, and vegetables, and was a major supplier for the eastern seed houses, such as Burpee's, that helped to put the Shakers out of the seed business. See Emma Burbank Beeson, *The Early Life and Letters of Luther Burbank* (San Francisco: Harr Wagner Publishing Co., 1927), pp. 69, 79.
6. Karl Schriftgiesser, "Harvard Shaker Colony Now a One Man Town," *Boston Evening Transcript*, 11 February 1925.
7. White and Taylor, *Shakerism*, p. 338.
8. [Harvard Ms January 1845–June 1852], Library of Fruitlands Museums.

9. William H. Dixon, *New America* (Philadelphia: J.B. Lippincott, 1867), p. 306.

10. Edward Deming Andrews, *The Community Industries of the Shakers* (Albany: The University of the State of New York, 1932), p. 259.

11. Virginia A. May, *A Plantation Called Petapawag* (Groton, Mass.: Historical Society, 1978), p. 146.

12. Marion Safford, "Facts and Fancies About the North Part of Lancaster," mimeographed [1921], pp. 12–13.

13. Frederick Sanderson, "Sanderson Family History," mimeographed, p. 80.

14. Sears, *Gleanings*, p. 296.

15. Elbridge Kingsley and Frederick Knabb, *Picturesque Worcester* (Springfield, Mass.: W.F. Adams Co., 1895), 2:85.

16. *Ibid.*, p. 83.

17. Chandler, *History of Shirley*, pp. 696–98.

18. *Ibid.*, p. 50.

19. Charles Dickens, *American Notes* (1842; reprint ed., Gloucester, Mass.: Peter Smith, 1968), p. 246.

20. Clara Endicott Sears passed on one dramatic, though perhaps fanciful, account, told her by Alonzo Willis, a carriage driver who boasted that he had helped a pair of lovers to flee the Shaker village at Harvard. A young man from Ayer took a liking to a Shaker sister during visits to the Shaker Sabbath service, and felt that she noticed him as well, though the two never spoke. One day he confided his attachment to Willis, insisting that he was enough in love to marry the girl. So Willis hatched a scheme to whisk her away as the Shakers emerged from their meeting house for the worship dance, which was sometimes conducted on the lawn. At the critical moment, the young man's courage failed, and Willis seized the girl, placed her in the carriage, and carried the two off to a waiting clergyman. The Shakers never came to "rescue" her, and the couple lived happily ever after. See "A Shaker Romance" formerly Monograph No. 111, an address delivered before the Harvard Historical Society at the home of Dr. and Mrs. Louis Cornish, June 21, 1938, pp. 1–3.

21. Pauline Wilkins, "The Shakers of Lovely Vineyard," *Worcester Sunday Telegram*, 26 March 1967.

22. William Dean Howells, "A Shaker Village," *Atlantic Monthly*, June 1876, p. 706.

23. Grosvenor United Society, 118 Mass.78 (1875), p. 78.

24. The exact nature of the doctrinal disagreement is unclear. Sears (*Gleanings*, p. 276) reports that the women left the Shakers in 1865 to study mesmerism; and Maria Fidelia is listed as subsequently establishing herself in the practice of this treatment at 28 Winter Street in Boston.

    An editorial in the *Oneida Circular* (prompted by a "long, sad" letter from the Grosvenors) expressed sympathy for the women. "Find-ing themselves in great want, with a bleak prospect ahead, and having received only $50 each at the time of expulsion, they brought suit. . . The hardship of these women consists . . . in the fact that the Shakers may have applied their legal rights too severely . . . If the women had voluntarily withdrawn from membership they would, perhaps, have had les claim to comassion. Still it may have been necessary to expel them to prevent their breeding insubordination and discontent in others." [Francis Wayland–Smith] ["Grosvenor Suit"], *Oneida Circular*, 12 (October 11, 1875), p. 324.

25. Sears, *Gleanings*, p. 276. The story was expanded upon during the years, and it was said that Grosvenor's disgrace extended to his even being forced to *sleep* with the swine. However, Harvard town histor-ian Elvira Scorgie rejected such notions, arguing that Grosvenor held other positions of honor following the Rural Home debacle. The broken heart remained on display at the Ayer drug store for some fif-teen years.

26. Marguerite F. Melcher, *The Shaker Adventure* (Princeton: Princeton University Press, 1941), p. 181. An account of Bennett's problems with the censor, Comstock, is also given in Gay Talese's *Thy Neighbor's Wife*, pp. 58–64.

27. Kingsley, *Picturesque Worcester*, p. 84.

28. Wilkins, *Worcester Sunday Telegram*, 26 March 1967.

29. Kingsley, *Picturesque Worcester*, p. 84.

30. Sears, *Gleanings*, p. 274.

31. "Visiting the Shirley Shakers," *Manifesto*, 19 (November 1889), pp. 257–58.

32. "The Shirley Shakers," *Manifesto*, 23 (December 1893), pp. 275–276.

33. Bolton, *Shirley Uplands*, p. 191.

Chapter 8: Struggle and Decline

1. "Shirley Records, 1842–1858," Harvard Historical Society.

2. John Davis Long, *America of Yesterday, As Reflected in the Journal of John Davis Long* . . . Edited by Lawrence Shaw Mayo . . . (Boston: The Atlantic Monthly Press, 1923), p. 115.

3. *Ibid.*, p. 116.

4. White and Taylor, *Shakerism*, p. 182.

5. John Whiteley, comp., "Letters and Documents Respecting the Con-scription, Arrest and Sufferings, Mental and Otherwise, of Horace S. Taber," mimeographed, Library of Fruitlands Museums.

6. The exchange of correspondence in the Taber case included, besides Taber and Whiteley, the names of ministry elders Grove B. Blanchard and William H. Wetherbee; trustees Jonas Nutting and Leander A.

Persons; family nurse Lucretia M. Godfrey; members Mary Y. Rodgers, William Pritchard, Abraham Whitney and Alpheus B. Davis; visitors John B. and Ellen Walker from Warren, Ohio; Nathaniel L. Kinsbury, Shirley physician prior to 1863; Isaac Kimball, justice of the peace, and Jerome Gardner, witness.

7. Thomas D. Clark, *The Kentucky* (New York: Farrar & Rinehart, 1942), p. 181.

8. Charles Nordhoff, *The Communistic Societies of the United States . . .* (New York: Harper & Brothers, 1875), p. 193.

9. Howells, "A Shaker Village," p. 704.

10. *Ibid.*, p. 709.

11. *Ibid.*, p. 710.

12. A Shirley ledger book ("Shirley Shaker Society Meals and Lodging Record Jan. 5, 1858–Dec. 10, 1891," in the Library of Fruitlands Museums), besides recording stops by Nordhoff of February 3, 1874, and the extended stay of Howells in 1875, shows visits by Hudson Maxim, an explosives inventor, on July 1, 1879, and E.L. Godkin, the influential founder of the weekly *Nation*, on July 24 of the same year.

   Distinguished callers included John Humphrey Noyes, celebrated as founder of the Oneida community and as author of *History of American Socialism*. Marianne Finch, author of *An Englishwoman's Experience in America*, lauded the Shirley Shakers for the quality of their applesauce. other societies had visits from Henry Clay, Andrew Jackson, James Monroe, Walt Whitman, Horace Greeley, Charles Dickens, Harriet Martiniau and Hepworth Dixon.

13. Although West's grandmother, Sister Catherine Walker, and his aunt, Eldress Annie Walker, were influential in the community, West never became a covenant member, pursuing instead a career in the world. He was active in town affairs, serving for a time as postmaster and as a member of the Harvard School Committee from 1905 to 1910. Well-spoken and possessed of a fine singing voice, he substituted occasionally for the minister at church services and sang at funerals, including those of the Shakers who died in the area after the community dissolved. He was married and had three children.

14. West, "Reminiscences," p. 351.

15. *Ibid.*, p. 353.

16. Charles Edson Robinson, *Concise History of the United Society of Believers Called Shakers* (East Canterbury, N.H., 1893), p. 122.

17. "Rules and Orders for the Church of Christ's Second Appearing Established by the Ministry of Elders of the Church Revised and Reestablished by the Same," (New Lebanon, New York, May 1860), Library of Fruitlands Museums.

18. West, "Reminiscences," p. 350.

19. Nordhoff, *Communistic Societies*, p. 192.

20. *Ibid.*, p. 194.
21. *Ibid.*, pp. 194–195.
22. *Ibid.*, p. 192.
23. Raymond B. Culver, *Horace Mann and Religion in the Massachusetts Public Schools* (New Haven: Yale University Press, 1929), p. 162.
24. Harvard (Mass.) School Committee, *Annual Report School Year 1881–82* (Ayer, Mass.: Printed at Public Spirit Office), p. 9.
25. "Shaker Anniversary," *Boston Globe*, 6 August 1896.
26. West., "Reminiscences," p. 357.
27. *Ibid.*, p. 358.
28. *Ibid.*, p. 359–60.
29. Bolton, *Shirley Uplands*, p. 191. One of Whiteley's guests caused much consternation in the community. The man, an overnight guest at the village, committed suicide by first taking poison and then slitting his throat with a razor. Whiteley noted that tragedy in a diary entry of April 26, 1899, and pasted an obituary clipping on the page. On the morning of the suicide, the man asked Whiteley to look in on him in his room before Whiteley left for Boston on business. Whiteley did so and the man wished him a hearty goodbye. Later in the day, Whiteley learned of the suicide in a telegram that interrupted him at his hotel in Boston. Whiteley wrote that the incident made "a great deal of trouble at the office." Two doctors came to view the body; they decided an inquest was not necessary. (See diary of John Whiteley, 1899, in the Library of Fruitlands Museums.)
30. Samuel A. Drake, ed., *The History of Middlesex County, Massachusetts* (Boston: Estes and Lauriat, 1880), p. 240.
31. "Journal of Maria Foster," Library of Fruitlands Museums.
32. "Visiting the Shirley Shakers," *The Manifesto*, (November 1899), pp. 257–58.
33. "Shakers' Anniversary," *Boston Globe*, 6 August 1896.
34. *Shaker Medicinal Spring Water* . . . (Boston, Mass.: [1881]), p. 13.
35. Sears, *Gleanings*, p. 278.
36. Evans emigrated to this country from his native England and became spokesman in the New Lebanon North Family. He made two lecture trips to England and engaged in a late-life correspondence with Count Leo Tolstoi. He tried to convert Tolstoi, get him to come to live at New Lebanon, and then to return to Russia to plant the seed of Shakerism. The sixty-year-old Russian author was intrigued but remained in Russia, brooding over the virtues of chastity while fathering his thirteenth child.
37. Melcher, *The Shaker Adventure*, p. 209.
38. Nordhoff, *Communistic Societies*, p. 161.
39. *The Manifesto*, 25 (April 1895), pp. 93–4.
40. *Worcester Telegram*, 27 April 1896.
41. *Ibid.*

42. *Public Spirit*, 19 April 1890.
43. "Rural Health Home, Ayer, Mass." [n.p., n.d.], Library of Fruitlands Museum.
44. *The Manifesto*, 27 (September 1897), p. 185.
45. "Rural Health Home," p. 1 and p. 4. Whether or not Watkins and his staff cured anybody is not recorded, but he probably made good on his boast that the "overworked and nervous can find rest and relaxation." A mouth-watering menu was listed, including wild game, oysters, lobsters, tender beef, turnips, peas, potatoes, pumpkin, and squash. Invalids were invited to sample the pure country air as well as Shaker spring water.
46. Letters to Rufus Bishop: later letters written by John Whiteley, Western Reserve Historical Society.
47. "Order and Succession of the Ministry, 1791–1835" and other lists of names, Shaker Collection, Western Reserve Historical Society, Cleveland.
48. "Shakers' Anniversary," *Boston Globe* 6 August 1896.
49. [Diary of John Whiteley, 1901], Library at Sabbathday Lake, Maine.

Chapter 9: Harvard and Shirley Closing

1. *Public Spirit*, 31 May 1902.
2. *Clinton* (Mass.) *Item*, 14 August 1905.
3. *Public Spirit*, 9 January 1904.
4. *Ibid.*, 28 December 1901.
5. *Ibid.*, 26 December 1903.
6. "Journal of Maria Foster," Library of Fruitlands Museums.
7. *Ibid.*
8. Clara Endicott Sears, Address to Bay State Historical League, Harvard Unitarian Church. July 22, 1939, Harvard Historical Society.
9. Norbert Weiner, *Ex-Prodigy: My Childhood and Youth* (New York: Simon and Schuster, 1953), p. 90.
10. Bolton, *Shirley Uplands*, p. 186.
11. Kingsley, *Picturesque Worcester*, p. 84.
12. (Ayer, Mass.) *Public Spirit*, 19 August 1905.
13. *Ibid.*
14. "Journal of Maria Foster," Library of Fruitlands Museums.
15. *Public Spirit*, 29 August 1908.
16. *Ibid.*, 24 October 1908.
17. Middlesex South Registry of Deeds, Book 3413, pp. 181–86.
18. *Records. Book No. 2.*, p. 88, New York Public Library (Manuscript and Archives Division).
19. *Ibid.*

20. *Fitchburg Sentinel* 26 October 1908.
21. Bolton scrapbook, Hazen Library.
22. "Journal of Maria Foster," Library of Fruitlands Musems.
23. "State Will Continue Work of Shakers," *Boston Globe* 19 September 1909.
24. Trustees Report of the Industrial School at Shirley, 1909–10, Massachusetts State Library, Boston.
25. "Shaker Colony Now One Man Town," *Boston Evening Transcript*, 11 February 1925.
26. "Journal of Maria Foster," Library of Fruitlands Museum.
27. *Records, Book 2.*, p. 96.
28. Clara Endicott Sears, "Inventory of the Shaker Museum 1941," pp. 12–13, Library of Fruitlands Museums, Harvard, Mass.
29. *Ibid.*, p. 10.
30. *Records. Book 2.*, p. 356.
31. Several weeks before the Shakers were to depart, on June 1, 1918, Frank and Edith were married by a clergyman in Cambridge. The marriage record lists Frank, 37, a farmer, of Harvard, and Edith, 36, of Concord. (Harvard Town Records.)
32. "Shaker Colony Now One Man Town."
33. *Records. Book No. 2.*, p. 356.

Chapter 10: The Ancient Landmarks

1. Warren was a graduate of Harvard College, national tennis champion in 1893, a world traveler, fighter for Philippine independence, and scion of a New England paper manufacturing family. Townspeople marveled at Warren's automobile exploits (he is said to have owned the first "horseless carriage" in Massachusetts) and his comings and goings on ocean liners to exotic ports. He was wealthy; the family business, still known as S.D. Warren Company with a plant operating in Westbrook, Maine, was purchased by Scott Paper Company. Warren also established the community of Halidon in Westbrook and Sant Jordi at Santa Coloma in the Republic of Andorra in Europe.
2. "Plan Farms For Ex-Soldiers on Site of Shaker Colony in Harvard," *Boston Sunday Globe*, 23 June 1923.
3. The mounting platform at the Shaker Museum came from the South Family *office building;* the platform that stood before the South Family *dwelling* was sold in 1932 and was moved to private property in Groton, where it remains.
4. "Shaker House Opened," *Public Spirit*, 11 June 1921.
5. Newcomb Green died on November 6, 1916, fatally stricken at age 70 after boarding a train at the Ayer depot.

6. *Public Spirit*, 7 December 1929.
7. "Sears Inventory of Shaker Museum," p. 16, Library of Fruitlands Museums.
8. Fruitlands Museums now also includes, in addition to the Alcott House and the Shaker House, an American Indian Museum and a Museum of American Folk Art, a reception center and library–administration building.
9. "Sears Inventory of Shaker Museum," p. 1.
10. Henrietta Jilson's married name was also Jilson, Henrietta having married one Frank Henry Jilson. The Jilson lineage is representative of the complex background and varied destinies of people who joined the Shakers. Henrietta and Eldress Josephine were two of the children of Abner Jilson and Caroline M. Potter, who were married in 1846. Their children, besides Henrietta and Josephine, were Charlotte, William Edward and Frank Abner. Following the father's death in 1853, the older children were placed with the Shirley Shakers and the mother kept her infant son, Frank. Henrietta and Charlotte left the Shirley community in their teens. Of the children, only Josephine remained with the Shakers. Henrietta married and had one child; Charlotte died at age 30; William married and had three children, and Frank married and had ten children.
11. The single Shirley cemetery monument replaced individual headstones in keeping with communistic ideals of the society. Elder Walter Shepherd, who presided at Eldress Josephine Jilson's funeral, later ordained that New Lebanon headstones be removed in favor of a single marker. This was one year before his own death and burial in January, 1933. Most, but not all, Shaker cemeteries followed this later practice.
12. "Pilgrimage to Shaker Village," *Public Spirit*, 19 August 1933.
13. *Public Spirit*, 24 September 1938.
14. Sears, *Gleanings*, p. 247.
15. Larry Anderson, "The Rural Home: It Broke Augustus Grosvenor's Heart," *Harvard Post*, 21 May 1976.
16. "History of Harvard 1894–1940," p. 199.
17. "Names and Places of Interment of Those Who Died at Harvard, 1784–1915," Shaker Collection, Western Reserve Historical Society, Cleveland.
18. "History of Harvard, 1894–1940," p. 199.
19. Robert Kimball, "Hancock Shaker Village Meetinghouse Didicated to Memory of Donor's Parents," *Berkshire Eagle*, 31 May 1963.
20. Federal Writers' Project, *Massachusetts: A Guide to Its Places and People* (Boston: Houghton Mifflin Company, 1937), p. 514.
21. The caretaker at the Woodlawn Cemetery was Frank Stanton. Stanton and his wife settled in Ayer after having helped the Shaker sisters move from Harvard to Mount Lebanon. Stanton worked as a

machinist most of his life after leaving the Shakers. Stanton and his wife attended the Federated Church and were active in the local lodge of Odd Fellows and its auxiliary, the Rebekahs. The couple had one child, a daughter. In 1963, Edith Hobbs Stanton died at age 81, and in 1967, Frank Stanton died, age 86. In 1979, the last of the children of Newcomb Green–Azel Green, grandson of Eldress Louisa Green–died in Ayer. All are buried in Ayer's Woodlawn Cemeter.

Meanwhile in Harvard, Arthur West died in 1937, and Dora Avery in 1964. Miss Sears lived to be 97, dying in 1960.

22. "Holy Hill Dedicated in Harvard," *Worcester Telegram*, 22 May 1976; also "Shaker Eldresses Visit Harvard for Holy Hill Dedication," *The Harvard Post*, 28 May 1976.

Chapter 11: Now and Tomorrow

1. C. Allyn Russell, "The Rise and Decline of the Shakers," *New York History* 49, No. 1 (January 1968) :48.
2. "TV Evening Magazine," WBZ, Boston, Mass., October 14, 1978.
3. Bishop, *Testimonies*, p. 186.
4. "All Things Anew," *Shaker Quarterly*, Winter 1972, p. 119–20.
5. Anna White and Leila S. Taylor, *Shakerism: Its Meaning and Message* (Columbus, Ohio: Press of Fred J. Heer, 1905), p. 393.
6. Robley Edward Whitson, *The Shaker Vision* (Canterbury, N.H.: Shaker Village, 1974), p. 13.
7. In 1835, the grave of Mother Lucy Wright was repositioned in the Shaker Common Burying Ground at Watervliet and the original grave sites of Mother Ann Lee, William Lee and one William Bigsby were relocated from the old cemetery to the newer cemetery. The Shakers kept as relics from Lucy's grave a lock of her hair, two teeth, and her hair pin. Mother Lucy had been dead fourteen years. Mother Ann had been dead fifty years and bones were found, including the skull, which showed evidence of fractures, perhaps from beatings. There was no mention of any of Mother Ann's or Father William's bones being reserved as relics prior to reinterment of the remains—at least in the account of an eyewitness. "Copy of a letter to Eldress Ruth Langdon on Exhuming, Removing and Re-interring the Remains of Mother Ann, W'm Lee and W'm Bigsby—By Buckingham 1835," Library at Sabbathday Lake, Maine.
8. *Dictionary of American Biography*, s.v. "Lee, Ann."
9. White and Taylor, *Shakerism*, p. 27.
10. Chandler, *History of Shirley*, p. 275.
11. *Notable American Women 1607–1950* Cambridge, Mass.: The Belknap Press, 1971), pp. 386–87.
12. Russell, "Rise and Decline," p. 50.

13. Stephen N. Howard, "Voices of the Shakers—Some Simple Rules," *Pegboard*, Fall 1979, p. 18.
14. "The Talk of the Town," *New Yorker*, August 5, 1974, p. 30.
15. Pam Robbins and Robley Whitson, "Gift from the Shakers," *Sign*, November 1979, p. 14. Though this Catholic magazine article celebrates early Shaker ecumenical sentiment, the Shakers joined in the internecine warfare so common among Christian denominations. As late as 1876—in *The Shaker*, April 1876, p. 32—Shaker columnists twitted the Vatican, writing, "The Pope's household numbered 1,160 persons . . . to which must be added the Sacred College."
16. Green *Summary View*, p. 35.

Index